SECRETS OF ANCIENT CULTURES

THE MAYA

SECRETS OF ANCIENT CULTURES

THE MAYA

Activities and Crafts from a Mysterious Land

Arlette N. Braman

Illustrated by Michele Nidenoff

WILEY

John Wiley & Sons, Inc.

Photo credits: Page 5 photo by Jean-Philippe Soule. Courtesy of www.nativeplanet.org. Page 9 copyright © 2001 by Bonampak Documentation Project. Reconstruction by Heather Hurst with Leonard Ashby. Page 71 copyright © 1976 by Merle Green Robertson.

Published by John Wiley & Sons, Inc., Hoboken, New Jersey
Published simultaneously in Canada

Design and production by Navta Associates, Inc.

The publisher and the author have made every reasonable effort to ensure that the experiments and activities in the book are safe when conducted as instructed but assume no responsibility for any damage caused or sustained while performing the experiments or activities in this book. Parents, guardians, and/or teachers should supervise young readers who undertake the experiments and activities in this book.

For general information about our other products and services, please contact our Customer Care Department within the United States at (800) 762-2974, outside the United States at (317) 572-3993 or fax (317) 572-4002.

Wiley also publishes its books in a variety of electronic formats. Some content that appears in print may not be available in electronic books. For more information about Wiley products, visit our web site at www.wiley.com.

Library of Congress Cataloging-in-Publication Data:

Braman, Arlette N., date.
   Secrets of ancient cultures : the Maya : activities and crafts from a mysterious land / Arlette Braman.
      p. cm.
   Summary: Provides a history of the ancient Maya civilization, as well as recipes, games, and directions for crafts based on Mayan culture.
   Includes bibliographical references and index.
   Contents: Daily life—Society—Food—Art and architecture—Science, math, and writing.
   ISBN 0-471-21981-9 (pbk. : alk. paper)
   1. Mayas—Material culture—Juvenile literature. 2. Maya cookery—Juvenile literature. 3. Creative activities and art work—Juvenile literature. [1. Mayas. 2. Maya cookery. 3. Handicraft.] I. Title.
F1435.3.M32 .B73 2004
972.81'016—dc21   2002032432

To Jill Decker,
one terrific present-day kid!

CONTENTS

ACKNOWLEDGMENTS

I would like to thank Michele Morgan, Ph.D., Associate Curator of Osteology, Peabody Museum of Archeology and Ethnology, Harvard University; Dr. Kevin Johnston for sharing his expertise on the Maya; Susan Feinberg, from the Maya Educational Foundation; Elaine González , an instructor and lecturer, and the author of *The Art of Chocolate,* for sharing her recipe for chili chocolate drink; chef Ruben López Ayala, Yaxche Maya Cuisine, Playa del Carmen, Mexico, www.mayacuisine.com, for giving me the recipe for chicken Pacal, and to Erica from Maya Cuisine, who helped me make the connection; Ignacio Hernandez Jr., mexgrocer.com, for answering all my chili questions; Lauren McCabe, who connected me to Katia Torres from Guatemala City, Guatemala; Sylvia Perrine, archivist, Foundation for the Advancement of Mesoamerican Studies, Inc., for directing me to experts in the field; Dr. Merle Greene Robertson, "Indiana Jane" of Maya studies and chairman of the board of the Pre-Columbian Art Research Institute for telling me about Dr. Mary Miller at Yale University, who allowed me to use one of her slides; David Greene, managing director of the Pre-Columbian Art Research Institute, for having the best Lord Pacal print; the people at the Textile Museum, Washington, D.C., for their help with Maya textiles; the folks at the Dumbarton Oaks Research Library and Collection, Washington, D.C.; and to Dr. Pat Pinciotti, East Stroudsburg University, for always helping me with my many last-minute requests.

A big thanks to Jill Decker and my kids, Callan and Abigail, for lending their activity-testing talents.

A note about the recipes: The recipes used in this book were all modified to make them easier for kids to use.

To buy food ingredients online, try these Web sites:

www.mexgrocer.com

www.ethnicgrocer.com

thecoolshopper.com/food.htm

Always check with an adult before buying ingredients online. Other Web sites referred to in this book were current at the time of publication.

Introduction
THE ANCIENT MAYA

The ancient Maya civilization was quite possibly the greatest of the New World civilizations. These brilliant people excelled in astronomy, mathematics, architecture, farming, and irrigation techniques, and they developed a fascinating culture that lasted almost 4,000 years. But when did this civilization begin and where did its people come from? Their ancestors had migrated from northern areas of the Americas to the vast region of what is present-day Guatemala, Mexico, Belize, El Salvador, and Honduras around 9000 B.C. They were hunters and gatherers who moved around according to seasonal changes to locate food and to find the best hunting and fishing. When a group of people stay put, build villages, and begin to cultivate the land, a complex civilization has a chance to grow and develop. Historians believe this is what happened with the ancient Maya. Around 2500 B.C., the early Maya began to cultivate **maize** (corn) and establish villages. Over time, some of these villages grew into

GEOGRAPHICAL ZONES

The homeland of the ancient Maya was a vast area divided into three major geographical zones.

The Pacific coastal plain lies along the Pacific coast, has a tropical climate, and provided the Maya who lived there with plenty of hunting and fishing opportunities. It was also good land for growing cacao.

The highlands offered the Maya the most diverse geography. This mountainous area includes the southern highlands and the northern highlands. The Maya obtained **obsidian** (a hard volcanic rock) and mined jade in this mineral-rich area. Volcanic eruptions could occur in the southern highlands, but the rich, fertile soil proved excellent for growing food.

The lowlands have a warm tropical climate, abundant limestone, and soil that was good for producing food. This area is divided into the southern and northern lowlands. The southern lowlands have many lakes, which provided the Maya with plenty of water for drinking, watering crops, and canoe travel. The northern lowlands have porous limestone, and surface water is scarce, but the Maya were able to find water in underground wells.

Gulf of
Mexico

Caribbean Sea

Mayapan
•
Chichén
Itzá
•
Uxmal
•
▲ Northern
Lowlands

•Tikal
•Palenque
▲Central Lowlands

Gulf of Honduras

Bonampak
•
▲ Southern
Lowlands

Pacific Coastal Plain

▲
▲ Northern
Highlands

•Copán

Pacific
Ocean

Southern
▲ Highlands

• Key cities

▲ Geographical zones

great cities. At its height, around A.D. 400–900, the empire of the Maya covered an enormous area from the northern plains of the Yucatán Peninsula of Mexico to the tropical jungle of Petén in Guatemala.

Maya history is classified into three major periods, which helps define how the Maya lived and what level of advancement they had achieved as a society.

The Preclassic Period (about 2500 B.C.–A.D. 200) Begins with the transition from nomadic hunter/gatherer groups to agricultural villages and ends with the planning of the great cities.

The Classic Period (200–900) This was a time of large-scale city building; major advancements in the arts, science, and agriculture; and large population growth.

The Postclassic Period (900–1521) At this time, many Maya cities in the southern lowlands were abandoned, while cities in the northern lowlands, such as Chichén Itzá, flourished. The end of this period marks the Maya's first encounter with the Spanish.

City-States

The Maya empire consisted of many city-states, each with its own king (also considered to be the high priest) and governors. At the heart of the city-states were

OTHER MESOAMERICAN CIVILIZATIONS

The Maya was just one of the advanced ancient civilizations that arose in **Mesoamerica** (Mexico and Central America). Here is a look at some of the other civilizations that lived in Mesoamerica before and after the Maya.

Olmec
An early Mesoamerican civilization who were artistically and technologically advanced, the Olmec produced massive stone sculptures, intricate water management systems, and large ceremonial centers. They emerged in the area between 1500 and 1200 B.C. and lasted until about 400 B.C.

Zapotec
These people were at the height of their civilization around 600 B.C. and dominated the Oaxaca region of what is now Mexico for more than 1,000 years. They are credited with developing one of the earliest writing systems.

Toltec
A major military force in Mesoamerica, they established their capital at Tula around A.D. 856 and dominated the area for the next two centuries.

Aztec
They rose to power in the Valley of Mexico in the fourteenth century A.D., establishing Tenochtitlán as their capital. By A.D. 1500, they were a powerful military group who acquired land through warfare.

MAJOR CITY-STATES

Tikal
One of the largest Maya city-states, it was a major center of Maya architecture. It is located in present-day Guatemala.

Uxmal
Located in the western Yucatán in present-day Mexico, this city had one of the largest Mesoamerican buildings—it was more than 300 feet (91 m) long.

Copán
This city was the center for astronomical study by Maya priests. It is located in present-day Honduras.

Palenque
Located in the highland rain forest of present-day Mexico, this city had some of the finest Maya sculptures. The Temple of Inscriptions to honor Lord Pacal is located here.

Chichén Itzá
This major center for Maya ball games, located in present-day Mexico, had seven ball courts. One may have been the largest in all of Mesoamerica. It also included a now famous building, an observatory called El Caracol, which has windows that align with Venus and the sun at certain times of the year.

Bonampak
This city was famous for its beautiful painted murals that depicted important events and major battles. *Bonampak* means "painted wall" in the Maya language. It is located in present-day Mexico.

ceremonial centers. Every aspect of Maya life revolved around these centers, which included palaces, pyramid-temples, observatories, ball courts, and monuments. Kings and their relatives, who made up the upper classes, lived in the ceremonial centers. People from the lower classes lived farther out from the centers of the city-states, but they came in for religious ceremonies, festivals, and ball games. The rulers of the city-states often fought among themselves to gain more land or get captives. Rulers needed these captives to work as laborers. Some also became human sacrifices to please the gods.

By 1517, the Maya had constructed 200 city-states. At least 20 of these cities had populations of over 50,000. Historians estimate that when the Maya civilization reached its peak between A.D. 600 and 900, as many as 20 million people may have lived in the region.

What Happened?

Around A.D. 900, the Maya civilization began to decline. Why did such a brilliant civilization seem to suddenly fail? Why did the southern lowland Maya cities virtually collapse in the Late Classic Period while the Maya cities in the northern lowlands went on to achieve greatness? Research points to three probable factors: warfare, overpopulation, and drought. These three key factors did not necessarily happen all at once, but all three quite possibly had a major impact on the decline of the lowland Maya cities. By 925, the southern lowland cities had been abandoned.

The northern lowland cities like Chichén Itzá flourished after this time, but by A.D. 1200 the city had collapsed. The Maya established new cities, such as Mayapán, but this city was constructed quickly with little planning, and it was destroyed in a battle in 1441. The Maya, now scattered about, tried to survive in small cities throughout the region.

In 1517, the first Spanish explorers arrived in Mesoamerica. Hernán Cortés, a Spanish nobleman, and 500 soldiers arrived two years later, hoping to find a fortune in gold and jewels. Cortés and his soldiers set out to conquer the region. The Spanish also brought European diseases, like smallpox, influenza, and measles, which killed an estimated one-third to one-half of the Maya population. The Maya continued to fight the Spanish, but by 1546, the Maya cultural dominance of the region was over.

Modern Maya

Although the Maya civilization declined, the Maya people did not disappear. Descendants of these ancient people struggled for years against Spanish domination to survive in the lands of their forefathers. Today there are more than 4 million Maya living in their original homeland in Guatemala, the Yucatán Peninsula of Mexico, Honduras, El Salvador, and Belize.

Though the Maya have adopted modern ways over the years, many Maya continue to practice the customs of their ancestors. The Dance of Resistance is still performed each year to remind the Maya of how their ancestors fought against the Spanish. The ancient religion is practiced along with Christianity. The people pray to the Maya gods for guidance in farming and other work, and they pray to Christian saints for guidance with family life. The Maya continue to speak the Mayan language, though some also speak Spanish and English. Many men still work in **milpas** (cornfields) as their ancestors did, and many women weave and make traditional clothes by hand. Maya children combine a modern life with tradition. Many take care of their younger siblings while their parents work. Boys help their fathers farm, while girls help their mothers at home. But like kids everywhere, Maya children love to have fun and play games, softball, soccer, or just hang out with their friends.

PART ONE

DAILY LIFE

The Maya lived in extended family groups, which means that parents, children, grandparents, and other relatives all lived very close to each other. Homes were built in family clusters, and each cluster had a patio that was shared by all the homes in the cluster. Everyone in the family helped with all the work. Men and older boys did the farming. They cleared and weeded the fields and planted the crops. When not farming, they hunted and fished. Maya women and older girls sewed the family's clothes, prepared and cooked the meals, raised the younger children, gathered firewood, and collected water from wells. If anyone in the family owned a slave, that person lived in the cluster as well.

A Maya Home

Family life for the average Maya was centered around the family plot of land, which included the home, a well, a **latrine** (outside bathroom), a chicken coop, and a garden where they might grow guavas, papayas, avocados, watermelon, and other foods for their own tables. Each village also had a communal plot of land that everyone in the village farmed.

The Maya used perishable organic materials to build their homes, so most of the ancient homes decayed over time. But archeologists have found some ruins of homes and believe that the homes of the ancient Maya were much like the rural houses made in the region today. Examples of Maya homes were also depicted in Maya writings, painted in murals, and carved into stone. The typical house was rectangular, had no windows, and contained only one room inside. Gravel and packed soil made up the floor. At night, the family slept on the floor on thin reed mats. The outside of the house was either made from stone or **adobe** (sun-dried clay) bricks or had a wooden construction of poles made from tree branches. Tree branches and palm fronds created a roof. The entry door faced east to greet the rising sun. Women cooked meals both inside and outside on a grill positioned over rocks. In tropical areas, the lowland Maya built their homes on platforms or mounds made of earth and stone to protect them from possible flooding after tropical storms.

Marriage

Maya marriages were arranged. A young man's family worked with a matchmaker to find the right young woman for their son. The matchmaker helped negotiate certain issues, such as how long the son-in-law would work for his father-in-law and what price the groom's family would have to pay for the bride. A Maya man generally married around the age of 18, and a woman usually between the ages of 14 and 15. A man generally had only one wife, but if he could afford it he could marry other women.

Before the ceremony, the couple consulted a priest, who chose a lucky day for the marriage date. The community built the couple a small house and supplied it with pottery for cooking, drinking gourds, and baskets. The ceremony was performed by a priest at the new home of the bride and groom. During the ceremony, the bride and groom sat on mats facing each other, watching the fire in the hearth that the priest had lit. After the ceremony, the priest left and the couple remained until the fire was out. The festivities for the guests continued back at the bride's family's home.

Divorce was allowed if the marriage did not work out, but no formal ceremony was needed. The couple simply stated that they were divorced.

DEATH RITUALS

Death terrified the Maya, but they believed that living a good life ensured a place in one of the 13 heavens. Some people were guaranteed a place in paradise, such as priests, women who died in childbirth, warriors killed in battle, and sacrificial victims. If you did not live a good life, you might go to the underworld, where you'd be forever tortured by demons.

The Maya usually buried their deceased relatives under the family house, then left the house for their grieving period. Before they buried the body, the relatives filled the deceased's mouth with maize so that he or she wouldn't be hungry on the journey to one of the heavens. The relatives then wrapped the deceased in cotton and placed a few personal items in the grave.

Time to Celebrate

Although daily life could be challenging, the ancient Maya loved celebrations and enjoyed many festivals over the course of a year. All classes of society took part in these celebrations, which were usually held in the large open plaza area of the city. Some celebrations had a sacred connection, while others were just for entertainment. Important events to celebrate included the birth of

an heir to the throne, a new ruler taking the throne, and the dedication of a temple.

The Maya held festivals every 20 days to celebrate the start of a new month. They also celebrated and made sacrifices during the changes of seasons to encourage the growth of crops. During these celebrations, the Maya upper class dressed in their fanciest clothes.

One of the most beautiful celebration scenes is a mural located at Bonampak. The scene depicts the announcement of King Chab-Muan's heir. The turquoise background is a perfect backdrop for the Maya dancers in brightly colored crayfish and caiman costumes. Musicians play drums, rattles, and trumpets to honor the newborn heir.

The ancient Maya enjoyed playing games and made rubber balls, using the sap from the rubber tree, long before Columbus arrived in the New World. They made and used rubber as early as 1600 B.C.

Religion

Religion governed all aspects of Maya life. The ancient Maya prayed daily to a variety of gods for good fortune and success in everything they did. If they were plagued by illness or had accidents, the Maya believed the gods were punishing them for not living a good life. The Maya believed that priests and kings were the only people who held special powers to communicate with the gods and

BLOODLETTING

Bloodletting, a ritual of offering one's own blood to the gods, was an important part of Maya life. The Maya used thorns, flint knives, or stingray spines to pierce their skin. They let the blood drip onto bark paper and then burned the paper. The smoke would carry the blood to the gods, which was the only way that gods could consume the blood. The Maya also believed that their dead ancestors and the gods could enter the physical world through a wound in the body. Bloodletting was done at weddings, funerals, religious holidays, and festivals.

the supernatural world. The Maya understood their world through religion.

The Maya worshipped many gods and believed that these gods inspired the Maya to accomplish great things. The gods could be both kind and unfriendly. They could change their appearance, change their role from day to night, and have more than one identity. The Maya believed that the gods lived in both the upperworld, which consisted of thirteen layers, or heavens, and was above the earth, and the underworld, which had nine layers and was located below the earth.

Only the priests could truly understand the gods and how to please them. Here are some of the main Maya gods:

Itzamná The god of creation who ruled the heavens and invented writing, math, and the calendar. He brought happiness to people.

Kinich Ahau The god of the sun who brought warmth and light to the people. He wanted nothing to do with sickness, wars, or other problems.

Ek Chuah The god of merchants. He protected those traveling through jungles or mountains to get to other villages.

Ix Chebel Yax The goddess of spinning, weaving, and dyeing, she was the wife of Itzamná.

Chaak The god of rain. He looked frightening with his fanglike teeth, but this god was kind. He brought water to the crops.

SACRED BOOK

One of the most remarkable among all the surviving Maya texts is the *Popol Vuh* of the Quiche Maya. Written shortly after the Spanish conquest, it recounts the Maya creation story and the adventures of the Hero Twins, Hunahpu and Xbalanque, who tricked and defeated the lords of the underworld.

AT WORK

The daily life of the average Maya woman was one of cooking, gardening, weaving, trading extra food at markets, and raising her children. She also had the responsibility of making all of her family's clothes, by spinning fibers, such as cotton and wool, into thread that she used for weaving cloth. Women sewed all of the clothes each family member needed, such as skirts, blouses, pants, and other garments, from rectangular strips of the woven cloth. Most of the clothes she made for her family were in natural colors and had little decoration. But clothes for the royals were decorated with colorful details. The cloth could be dyed, hand painted, or stamped

The Maya believed in a strict dress code. Anyone who violated this dress code could be put to death. The type of cloth, its color and design, and its size and shape, as well as headdresses and shoes, all signified social rank. For example, upper-class men wore a square cotton cloth around their shoulders that was colorful and was decorated with designs and feather work. Men from the lower class wore the same piece of clothing, but with little or no color or decoration.

with dye to create designs. The Maya also used embroidery and brocading on special clothes, and sometimes attached shells, feathers, or precious stones.

Although no ancient Maya clothing exists today, we know much about these ancient clothes from the fragments that have been found. Archeologists have been able to piece together parts of the clothing puzzle by studying these fragments as well as pictures of clothing on Maya vessels, murals, clay figures, sculpture, and texts.

Ancient Textiles

The Maya grew cotton that women spun into thread and wove into cloth. To add warmth to the cloth, rabbit hair was sometimes spun with the cotton. Some clothes were made from other materials, such as *ixtle* fibers from the **agave**

(a succulent plant related to the lily family). Another important fiber was from the *chichicaxtle* plant. Finer in texture than *ixtle,* cloth made from *chichicaxtle* most closely resembled our linen, which is spun from the fibers of the flax plant.

Maya women in all classes of society wore the same items of clothing, though clothes for upper-class women were colorful and had fancy designs:

Wraparound skirt

Waist sash (This held the skirt in place.)

Oversized blouse or *huipil*

Cape or *quechquemitl*

Sandals made from deer hide or *ixtle* (Many women went barefoot. The ruling class wore jaguar-skin sandals for special occasions.)

Mantle (A long piece of cloth draped over the head and used as a sling to carry babies or other items.)

Decorating Techniques

Maya women used a variety of techniques to enhance the look of the clothing worn by the upper classes. Here are some of the more common techniques used:

Freehand painting: Designs were painted on cloth with animal-hair brushes.

Fabric printing: A clay or stone seal onto which a design had been carved was dipped in dye and used to print the design on the cloth.

◆ CLOTHES FOR MEN ▷

As with women, clothes for Maya men in all classes of society included similar items, but clothes for the upper-class were more colorful and decorative:

Loincloth (A long piece of cloth wrapped around the waist, passed between the inner thighs, then tied to secure it in place. Sometimes the ends hung in the front and back of the body. Depending on social rank, these could be decorated with fancy designs.)

Pants (Simple in style and gathered around the waist. The pants could be worn in place of a loincloth.)

Vest (Tight, sleeveless top, open at the front and ending at the top of the thighs. Worn with pants.)

Cape (Knotted in the front and at the sides.)

Netted cape (Nobles wore this fishnet-like cape over their fancy cloth capes.)

Sandals made from deer hide or *ixtle* (The ruling class wore jaguar-skin sandals for special occasions.)

Plangi: Similar to tie-dyeing. Sections of cloth were tied in a way that prevented dye from coloring those sections. Sometimes a design was drawn on the cloth before dyeing.

Ikat: The threads were dyed before weaving instead of after. Sections of the threads were tied in a way to prevent them from being dyed when dipped in the dye bath. To achieve a multicolored look, different sections of threads could be tied before being dipped in a new color.

Brocade: A raised design created by weaving threads into the fabric.

Embroidery: Threads are sewn onto a finished woven fabric to create designs. The Maya used copper and bone needles for stitching.

PLANGI SHIRT

Ancient Maya women used the plangi, or tie-dyeing, method to produce colorful clothes with interesting patterns and designs. It was quite an art to produce these clothes. Using store-bought dye and a T-shirt, you can replicate this ancient method for dyeing your shirt. You can paint an ancient Maya design on your shirt after it is dyed.

SUPPLIES

- white 100% cotton T-shirt, your size or larger
- 15 to 20 thick rubber bands
- 1 bottle of liquid Rit dye in any color
- 1 cup salt (optional)
- measuring cup

- rubber gloves
- 1 large plastic container
- hot water
- scissors
- liquid clothes detergent
- craft fabric paint in a variety of colors
- paintbrush

STEPS

Note: Adult help may be needed.

1 Lay the shirt out on a flat surface. Starting at one long side of the shirt, fold the shirt like an accordion.

2 Starting at one end of the folded shirt, wrap a rubber band around the folded shirt every 2 inches (5 cm) as shown. (If a rubber band breaks, you can use another,

or just wrap it around the shirt and tie the ends together.) Set the shirt aside.

3 Put on the rubber gloves and place the plastic container in the sink in case of splashes. Prepare your dye bath in the plastic container by following the directions on the dye bottle. You will need hot water and you may need to add the cup of salt, but check the directions on the dye bottle before doing this.

4 Once your dye bath is ready, place the shirt in the dye bath and let it soak for about 15 minutes, moving it around constantly. (Note: if the color appears dark after less than 15 minutes, remove the shirt.)

5 Pour the dye down the drain, rinse out the container, place it on the counter, and place the shirt in the sink. Rinse the shirt under cool running water until the water coming from the shirt is clear. Squeeze the shirt to get as much water as possible out of the shirt.

6 Ask an adult to help you cut the rubber bands from the shirt, or if you do it yourself, be careful not to cut yourself or the shirt.

7 Place a very small amount of liquid detergent in the container and fill it with warm water. Place the shirt in the container, and wash it. Rinse the shirt under cool running water until it is soap free. Hang the shirt to dry.

8 After the shirt is dry, paint any of the designs shown below on your shirt.

ACCESSORIES

The Maya also loved to decorate their hair, teeth, and bodies. Both men and women braided strips of colored leather into their hair and often added feathers and jewelry to the braided strips. The Maya filed their teeth in different patterns and sometimes even had their front teeth inlaid with bits of jade. The upper classes wore earrings, rings in their lower lips, nose pieces, and bracelets and necklaces made of shells, turquoise, jade, rock crystals, and sometimes gold. Archeologists have found a wealth of beautifully crafted Maya jewelry.

AT HOME AND AT PLAY

After a Maya couple married, they looked forward to having children. To ensure this event, the wife said special prayers and placed an image of the goddess of childbirth, Ix Chel, under her bed. Once a child was born, everyone celebrated with a variety of ceremonies.

Name Giving

After the birth of a child, a priest came to give the child his or her name, which was in honor of the child's birthdate on the calendar. This date also determined the child's **horoscope** (astrological forecast), which the priest discussed with the parents to help them with child rearing. In all, a child received four names: *paal kaba*, the given name; the father's family name; *naal kaba*, the father's and mother's family names combined; and *coco kaba*, a nickname.

Signs of Beauty

Immediately after a child was born, the mother tied two boards to the front and back of the baby's head and left them there for a few days to flatten the forehead and the back of the head. The Maya considered a sloping head to be a sign of beauty. Maya mothers tied a small bead to the child's hair, which hung down on the child's forehead. When the child repeatedly looked at the bead, the result was crossed eyes. This was another sign of beauty.

Rite of Passage

When a child was about four years old, his or her parents began the process for the rite of passage into adulthood. They would tie a string with a red shell around a girl's waist and braid a white bead into a boy's hair. The shell and the bead would remain there until, at age 12 for girls and 14 for boys, the rite of passage ceremony was performed by a priest. An **elder** (a person in authority because of age) from the community was chosen as a sponsor and to provide a feast for the children who would be participating in the ceremony. Four other elders were chosen to assist the priest and the sponsoring elder. The ceremony took place in the courtyard of the elder's house. Children had to confess their sins, if any; then the priest said prayers, and the four elders placed pieces of white cloth on the children's heads. The child's sponsoring elder tapped the child's forehead with a bone and then moistened with water the child's forehead, face, and the spaces between the fingers and toes. After this, the priest removed the white cloths from the children's heads and cut the beads from the boy's hair. Finally, each mother cut the red shell from the girl's waist. Parents gave the children gifts and everyone feasted and celebrated. This ceremony made girls and boys eligible for marriage.

Time to Play

Maya children had little time to play after the age of about eight because they went to work in the fields or in the home. However, younger children were expected to do what most children do, and that was to play. They particularly enjoyed a kind of toy animal, such as a dog or a jaguar, that was shaped

from clay and had wheels. Toys with wheels have been found in Maya graves, and were possibly put there so the deceased child would have something to play with in the afterlife. Although the Maya used wheels for toys, they never used them for transportation. No one knows for sure why, but it may have been because the Maya had no pack animals to pull carts or wagons.

WHEELED TOY

To make a replica of a Maya toy, you need only a few items. Choose your favorite animal as your wheeled toy or make a dog or a jaguar, as the Maya did.

SUPPLIES

- self- or water-hardening craft clay
- 2 wooden dowels, 12 inches long by $1/4$ inch thick (30.5 by 1 cm)
- ruler
- pencil
- scissors
- water
- bowl
- glue
- craft acrylic paint, any color
- craft paintbrush
- paper towels

STEPS

1 Decide on the animal you'd like to make. From the clay, you will need to make a body, 4 legs, a head, 2 ears, and a tail. Mold each of these parts separately. The body should measure about $3\frac{1}{2}$ to 4 inches (9 to 10 cm) long and about 2 inches (5 cm) wide. The legs should be about 2 inches long (5 cm) by $\frac{3}{4}$ inches (2 cm) thick. You will need to mold a head in proportion to the rest of the body.

2 Measure and mark two $4\frac{1}{2}$-inch (11.5-cm) pieces from one of the dowels. *Ask an adult to help you cut the pieces on the marks.* You shouldn't cut all the way through the wood. Just make enough of an indentation so that you can break the piece off at the mark. Carefully push one of the dowels through the bottom of the leg as shown. Rotate the dowel to make the hole slightly larger than the thickness of the dowel. Do this for all the legs. Remove the dowel.

Push dowel through bottom of leg and rotate to make hole slightly larger than dowel's thickness.

3 Measure and mark two $2\frac{1}{2}$-inch (6-cm) pieces from the other dowel and have an adult help you cut as in Step 2. Carefully push the dowels through the front and back of the body. Attach the top part of the legs to the body by carefully pushing them through the dowel ends as shown.

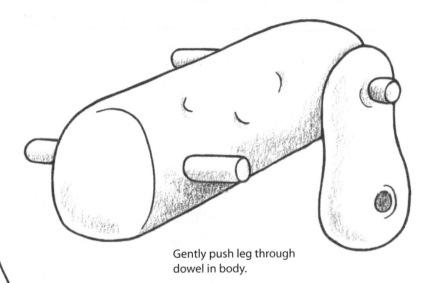

Gently push leg through dowel in body.

Always use moist fingers when you attach parts, smoothing all lines and cracks in the clay. Smooth small pieces of clay over the dowel ends to cover them after you attach the legs.

4 Attach the ears to the head by pushing the clay pieces together and smoothing the lines and cracks.

5 Measure one 2-inch (5-cm) piece of dowel and have an adult help you cut as in Step 2. Set this piece aside. Use a small piece of clay for the neck. It's easier to attach the head to the body using a neck. Carefully push the dowel you just cut into the base of the head just enough so that it does not come out the top of the head. Attach the head by pushing the other end of the dowel down into the neck and body. Smooth all cracks and lines in the clay to attach the head securely.

6 Attach the tail by pushing the clay pieces together and smoothing the lines and cracks. (Note: A shorter tail is less likely to break off after the clay hardens.)

7 Let your animal harden in a standing position according to the directions that came with your clay. In the meantime, make the wheels by molding four clay discs, each with a diameter of about $1\frac{1}{2}$ inches (4 cm) and a thickness of about $\frac{1}{4}$ inch (1 cm). Gently pat the edges of each wheel to make the edges a bit rounded. Use one of the $4\frac{1}{2}$-inch (11.5-cm) dowels to poke a hole in the center of each wheel. Rotate the dowel so that the hole becomes slightly bigger than the diameter of the dowel. Set the wheels aside to dry.

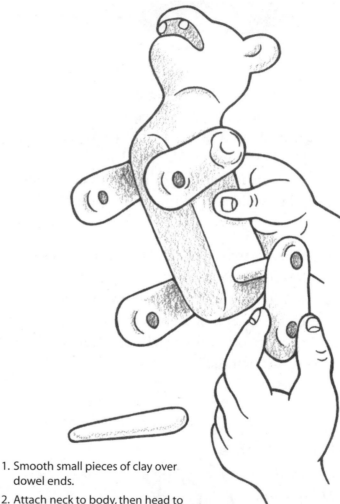

1. Smooth small pieces of clay over dowel ends.

2. Attach neck to body, then head to neck. Make sure to push dowel into base of head before attaching head to body.

8 Push the two 4½-inch (11.5-cm) dowels through the holes in the bottoms of the legs. Put the wheels on the ends of the dowels. Glue a small piece of clay on the end of each dowel to act as a stopper so the wheels won't fall off. These end pieces need to be bigger than the holes on the wheels. Let this clay harden.

9 Paint your animal and let it dry.

Maya Games

Many Mesoamerican cultures, including the Maya, played games, some of them with game boards. Evidence of square- and oval-shaped boards has been found carved in benches, on floors of stone buildings, and in the bases of monuments. Games were played both for fun and for more serious reasons. People may have even lost their freedom in games of chance.

Corn Game

The Maya enjoyed a game called *bul,* also known as the corn game. Players lined up corn kernels on the ground and used the spaces between the kernels for play. Other kernels with one side burned black were used as dice. *Bul* appears to have been a "war" game since players tried to capture or kill all of their opponent's game pieces.

It is believed to be an ancient board game, but no evidence of a *bul* board has ever been found in any ancient ruins, and there is no mention of this game in Maya writings. However, the word *bul* has been found in several Maya **dialects** (regional varieties of language that have different features from other varieties of the same language) and drawings of priests throwing corn kernels or seeds have also been found. It is possible the Maya never used a board but played the game wherever it was convenient.

PLAY BUL!

You can play *bul* as the ancient Maya did, making your own board from oaktag and using coins or other objects around your house as game pieces. Or, you can get creative and make Maya warriors out of clay to use as game pieces.

Number of Players: 2

Object of the game: To capture all of your opponent's game pieces.

SUPPLIES

- 1 piece of oaktag, about 9 by 24 inches (23 by 61 cm)
- ruler
- pencil
- scissors
- permanent markers, any color
- elbow macaroni, 4 pieces
- 10 objects for game pieces (5 of one object, such as pennies, and 5 of another, such as nickels)
- self- or water-hardening craft clay (optional)
- small bowl of water (optional)
- acrylic paint, any color (optional)
- paintbrush (optional)
- paper towels (optional)

STEPS

1 Measure and mark a 20½-by-5-inch (52 by 13 cm) section of the oaktag. Draw 13 lines spaced 1½ inches (4 cm) apart across the board.

2 Trace over these lines with a marker to make the lines thick. Using the markers, color the spaces of the board any colors you like. Then cut out the board and set it aside.

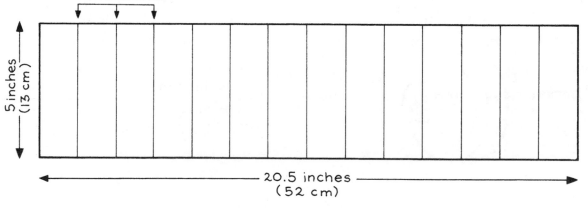

1.5 inches (4 cm) between lines

5 inches (13 cm)

20.5 inches (52 cm)

3 If you want to make clay playing pieces, mold a simple "warrior" in the shape of a pyramid no more than 2 inches (5 cm) high by about 1 square inch (2.5 cm) wide at the base. Keep your fingers moist while shaping the clay. You will need 10 game pieces in total. Let the pieces dry completely, then paint 5 in one color and 5 in a different color. Let the paint dry completely. If you use objects such as coins instead of the clay pieces, give 5 of the same coin to your friend and keep the other 5 for yourself.

4 Mark one side of each piece of elbow macaroni with a black marker. These are your dice. Set these aside to let the marker ink dry.

How to Play

1 Place the game board between you and your friend. Players each take 5 of the same color game pieces and set their pieces at opposite ends of the game board as shown.

2 Decide who goes first. That player takes the macaroni pieces and tosses them to get a score. Here's how to score:

1 black side up equals 1 move

2 black sides up equals 2 moves

3 black sides up equals 3 moves

4 black sides up equals 4 moves

4 unmarked sides up equals 5 moves

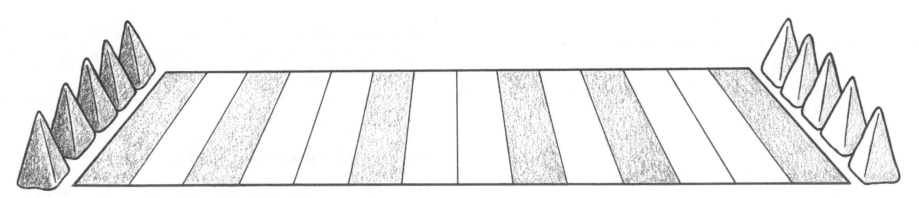

That player moves his or her warrior the number of spaces shown by the toss of the macaroni. Each player gets two tosses per turn, so the same player takes another turn. (Note: You play with only one warrior at a time until that warrior gets captured. Then you can use another one of your warriors.)

3 The next player tosses the macaroni and moves his or her warrior, then tosses again and moves again. The object of the game is to capture the other player's warriors. If one player's warrior lands on the space that is occupied by the other player's warrior, that warrior is "captured" and removed from the board. The player who lost a warrior may use one of his or her remaining warriors. The warrior who did the capturing may continue advancing on the board if it is still his or her turn.

4 When a warrior gets to the end of the game board without being captured, it is returned to its original starting place and continues until either it captures an opponent's warrior or is captured.

BUL ON-LINE

If you'd like to play the game on-line, go to this Web site and give it a try: http://www.halfmoon.org/bul.html

5 Continue playing until one player has captured all of his or her opponent's warriors. That player is the winner.

DANGEROUS GAME

Another game the ancient Maya played was the game of skill called *tlachtlic*. This was a kind of ball game played in a large court. Drawings of these courts have been found in codices. *Tlachtlic* was popular from 1500 B.C. to A.D. 1200. This dangerous game pitted two teams against each other, the object being to get a hard rubber ball through an elevated ring using only the hips, thighs, and elbows. Teams wore protective clothing such as helmets, gloves, knee pads, and hip protectors, since the game was quite physical. The losing team could lose more than their land, personal possessions, or pride. They could lose their lives. Human sacrifice was the result of many lost games. So important was this Maya game that it was mentioned in the sacred book *Popol Vuh*.

Musical Instruments

The Maya made a variety of instruments that they played as part of a celebration or to accompany dances. Ceremonial instruments included rattles, drums, flutes, long trumpets, whistles, and bells. Sun-dried gourds made perfect rattles.

Armadillo shells filled with dried melon seeds also worked as rattles. Artists also made rattles from clay, and often shaped them in the forms of animals. Carved wood and cleaned **conch** (large spiral-shelled mollusk) shells were used as trumpets. Flutes could be carved from wood or made from clay, and took many different shapes. Some drums were made from clay that was decorated with painted scenes. The open end of the drum was covered with a piece of animal skin stretched tightly across the top. Other drums were made from turtle shells. The musician used deer antlers as drumsticks.

The Maya used music in wartime as well. They blew conch shells and wooden trumpets at the start of a battle.

Ancient Whistles

The ancient Maya made many types of whistles. One favorite was a clay whistle in the shape of an animal, such as a toucan, turtle, or armadillo. The Maya were not the only ancient civilization to make these whistles. Other pre-Columbian cultures, such as the Aztec and Inca, as well as the ancient Chinese and ancient Egyptians, also made this instrument.

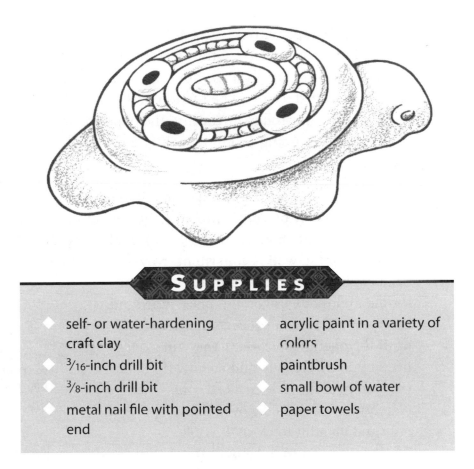

 ANIMAL WHISTLE

Follow these directions to make a whistle in the shape of an animal.

 SUPPLIES

- self- or water-hardening craft clay
- 3/16-inch drill bit
- 3/8-inch drill bit
- metal nail file with pointed end
- acrylic paint in a variety of colors
- paintbrush
- small bowl of water
- paper towels

STEPS

1 Decide on an animal for your whistle. Start with a ball of clay about 1 1/2 inches (4 cm) in diameter. Carefully

mold one end of the clay by gently pulling on it until it is a pointed shape with a rounded tip. Place the shaped clay ball on a flat surface with the pointed end resting down and gently press the clay on the surface. This slightly flattened part will be the top of the whistle. Slowly push your index finger into the opposite end of the clay ball, stopping about $1/2$ inch (1 cm) from the pointed end.

2 Use your thumb and index finger to enlarge the inside of the ball of clay by gently pressing the wall of the clay to a thickness of about $1/4$ inch (.5 cm). Make sure the thickness of the wall is consistent. Now the opening needs to be closed. Make a circle with your thumb and index finger and place it around the opening. Slowly squeeze this area until the opening is closed. You will need to do this slowly and evenly. If you can't get the hole to close completely, place some clay over the hole and blend it to close the hole. Wet your finger, then smooth it over the area where the opening was to seal it. Gently smooth the entire surface of the whistle. You may need to gently flatten the top part of the whistle again.

3 To make the air hole, find the place where the pointed end and the body of the whistle meet. Measure $1/4$ inch (.5 cm) back from that spot along the top of the whistle. At that spot use the $3/16$-inch drill bit to make a hole down into the cavity of the whistle. As you make the hole, gently rotate the drill bit. (Note: Use only a drill bit to make the hole. The excess clay will cling to the

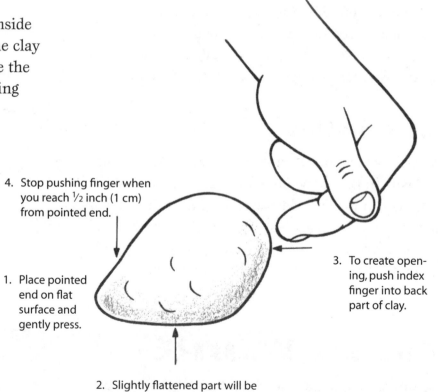

4. Stop pushing finger when you reach $1/2$ inch (1 cm) from pointed end.

1. Place pointed end on flat surface and gently press.

3. To create opening, push index finger into back part of clay.

2. Slightly flattened part will be top of whistle.

grooves in the drill bit and will not drop into the cavity, which you don't want to happen.) Once you are sure you have drilled into the cavity, use the $^3/_8$-inch drill bit to make the hole a little larger.

Use the nail file to angle the bottom rim of the hole as shown.

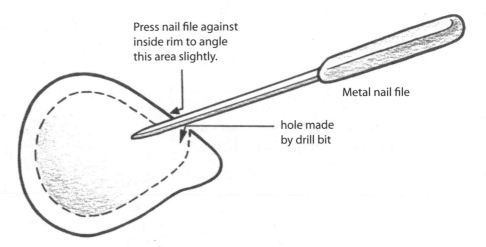

Press nail file against inside rim to angle this area slightly.

Metal nail file

hole made by drill bit

3. Measure $^1/_4$ inch (.5 cm) back from where pointed end and body meet. At that spot, gently push the $^3/_{16}$-inch drill bit straight down into the body of the whistle.

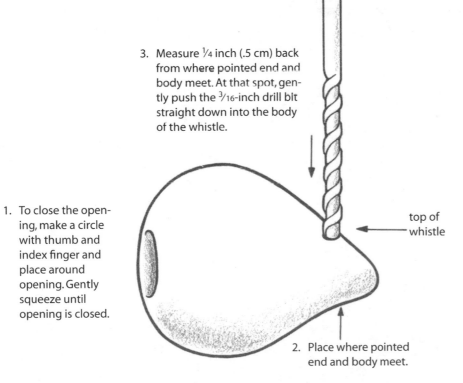

top of whistle

1. To close the opening, make a circle with thumb and index finger and place around opening. Gently squeeze until opening is closed.

2. Place where pointed end and body meet.

4 To create the mouthpiece hole, slowly push the nail file into the pointed whistle tip, stopping at the top edge of the air hole. The nail file should be angled exactly as shown. Try to remove any clay stuck to the end of the

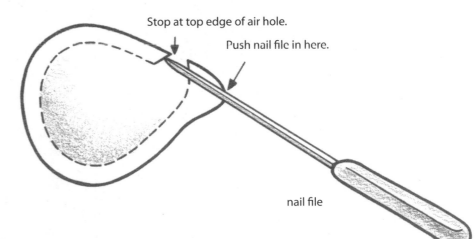

Stop at top edge of air hole.

Push nail file in here.

nail file

nail file before sliding it out. Try not to let the bits of clay drop into the cavity of the whistle. Make sure the airway is clear of any bits of clay.

5 Test your whistle by lightly blowing into the mouthpiece hole. Don't get discouraged if it doesn't whistle at first. You might need to make adjustments with the air and mouthpiece holes. If it doesn't whistle at all, you might want to start again. Let the whistle harden according to the directions that came with your clay. Paint your animal whistle any color you like. Let the paint dry completely.

SOCIETY

The Upper Class

Ancient Maya society had two classes. They consisted of the elite or upper class, and the nonelite, or lower class. Divisions existed within each class that determined a person's status. In the elite class, the king had the highest status. This noble ruler inherited the position. When he died, he passed the position down to the next male in line, preferably his son. If the king had no son, a brother or even the ruler's wife could take the throne. Kings and their families did not have to pay taxes. They ate the best foods, wore the most elaborate clothes, lived in palaces, had slaves, and never had to labor.

Under the king were a variety of other elite positions, some more important than others. Chieftains acted much like governors, enforcing local law and acting as judges for criminals. Administrative assistants and other lower-ranking elite government officials presided over public meetings and conducted rehearsals for festivals and dances. Many of these lower-ranking elite positions were appointed rather than inherited.

Priests were high-ranking members of the elite society. Priests helped the king rule and were in charge of religion. They were educated and powerful, and they read the stars, made predictions, conducted ceremonies, taught royal children, and were doctors. The priests were the only people in society who could read the calendars.

Other members of the upper class included warriors, merchants, architects, scribes, and artists. All of these people lived a privileged life to different degrees. The higher the status, the greater the privileges.

The Lower Class

Farmers made up the largest group in the lower class. They had the job of growing food for their families and for everyone in the upper class. Also in this class were the skilled craftsmen who made clothes and jewelry for the upper class. They built houses and temples and worked for the nobles. Unskilled laborers, slaves, and captives were at the bottom of this class.

People in this class were required to pay tribute to the rulers by giving them food they grew, honey, beeswax, woven cloth, fish, **game** (animals caught in hunting for food or sport), shells, and cacao. The rulers also required these people to give a certain amount of their time to help build roads, nobles' houses, palaces, temples, and other buildings. The nonelite made up the bulk of the population. Although this class never enjoyed the privileged life, rulers generally made sure the basic needs of these people were met.

FARMERS

The ancient Maya were skilled farmers. They planted a variety of crops, including maize, peppers, cacao, beans, tomatoes, squash, cotton, and fruits. Because the land they inhabited was so diverse, the Maya created a variety of farming methods for maximum food production and soil conservation.

Terraced Farming

On the slopes of volcanic mountains, the Maya farmers used a terraced farming system. They created graduated rows of flat-topped earth descending like steps from the top to the bottom of the slope. Terraced farming increased the amount of land available for growing crops and allowed for better drainage of excess water. With less soil erosion, more crops could be produced to feed the people.

Raised Field

Another method that proved successful, especially in swampy or flood-prone areas, was the raised-field technique. Rectangular raised fields were created by digging up dirt and piling it up in this rectangular area. This building-up process resulted in natural canals around the fields that held water needed to irrigate the field area and also promoted drainage. Animals and plants that lived in and around the canals produced organic matter that helped fertilize the fields. The Maya grew several types of crops in these raised fields, including corn, beans, and squash.

Slash and Burn

There is some evidence that Maya farmers used a slash-and-burn method of farming, by clearing a plot of land and then burning off the trees, leaving the ashes to fertilize the soil. In

the spring, the farmer sowed the seeds for the cornfield, or milpa. This method worked for about two to three years, but it stripped the soil of all its nutrients after that. The farmer had to then find another section of land to slash and burn, starting the cycle again. How do we know that the Maya may have used slash-and-burn agricultural methods? Traces of carbon, which is an element found in plant ashes, have been found in layers of soil that experts have analyzed.

SIMPLE TOOLS

Maya farmers did not use plows or have pack animals to pull plows. Instead, they used simple tools made from wood and stone. They used handmade hoes to break up the earth, and digging sticks—long pointed sticks used to make holes in the ground for the seeds. Today, some Maya farmers continue to use digging sticks.

Natural Wells

In the lowlands of the Yucatán Peninsula, groundwater was scarce during the dry season, so people had to rely on underground wells, called cenotes, for drinking water and irrigation. A **cenote** is a circular sinkhole created underground by the collapse of caves. Water in underground rivers seeped through the porous limestone walls of these natural wells, filling them with water. These wells were so important to the

survival of the Maya that people constructed villages close to them. If the well was particularly deep, the Maya had to use ladders made from rope of twisted vines. They carried large clay jugs down the long ladders, filled them with water, then carried them back up. The great city of Chichén Itzá was built around a cluster of these natural wells.

A Sacrificial Well

According to some experts, the Sacred Cenote, in Chichén Itzá, which was 65 yards (59 m) in diameter, was used only for sacrifices to the water god, Chaak. It is believed people were thrown into the well alive. During excavations of the well in 1901, the American archeologist Edward Thompson found more than 50 skeletons, many of which were men. Some children and a few young women were also identified. In addition, Thompson excavated gold, jade, and other artifacts from the bottom of the well. Some of the recovered items are on display in the Peabody Museum at Harvard University, but many have been returned to the Mexican government.

One group of archeologists believes that the bodies at the bottom of the Sacred Cenote fell in by accident and were not sacrificed. They use the argument that the Maya would not have polluted their own water supply. However, there is a Maya legend that says anyone who survived the well sacrifice in the Sacred Cenote would be treated as one who talked with the gods and was given special privileges.

ARTIFICIAL CENOTES

Cenotes did not exist in the northern part of the Maya empire. Getting water became a major challenge for the Maya in this region. To solve this problem, the Maya constructed thousands of underground **cisterns** (artificial reservoirs for water) to capture rainwater.

PLANT A FELD

In this activity, you will create a miniature raised field with canals and use it to grow herbs.

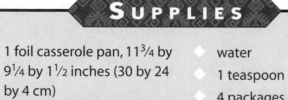

SUPPLIES

- 1 foil casserole pan, 11¾ by 9¼ by 1½ inches (30 by 24 by 4 cm)
- a handful of small stones
- 1 small bag of all-purpose potting soil, about 4 dry quarts (4 l)

- water
- 1 teaspoon
- 4 packages of herb seeds, such as dill, chives, basil, or rosemary

STEPS

1 Since this part is messy, do this first step outside or in a work area of the house. *Note: Check with an adult before starting, and wear old clothes.* Place the stones in a single layer in the bottom of the pan. If you have too many, remove some. Fill the pan with soil to just below the top rim. Add some water to moisten the soil. It may take a few minutes for the soil to absorb the water. Use the spoon to mix the water and soil together or use your hands. The soil should be moist and hold together, but it should not be soaking wet. The soil will sink down in the pan a little.

2 After you have moistened the soil, use the spoon handle to create canals in the soil. Do this by "cutting" two sections of the soil apart, as if you were cutting a cake. Make one vertical cut and one horizontal cut. Then move the spoon handle back and forth in the cut area to separate the sections of soil, leaving a space, or canal, between them. (You can also use your fingers to push the canal soil back into the platform of soil.) If any of the soil falls from the raised platform of soil, put it back on the platform and gently pat it.

3 Use 1 herb package per raised platform. Sprinkle the seeds on the raised platforms of soil.

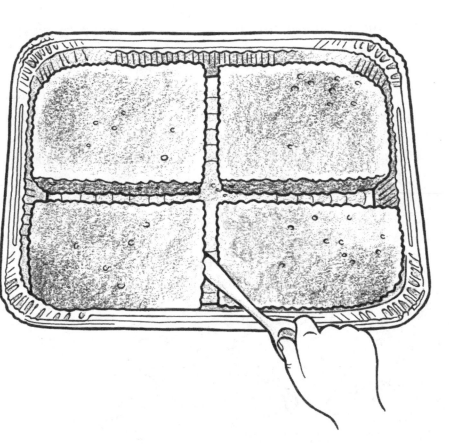

Make spaces in the dirt to create canals.

4 Lightly cover the platforms with more soil. Gently pat this soil in place. Lightly water the platforms. Some of the soil will fall into the canals. Use the spoon handle to scoop it up and place it back on top of the platform. You may need to use your fingers to push the platforms apart, keeping the canals open. Some water will drain into the canals, but this is okay.

5 Place the foil pan in a sunny area in your house. When you water, pour the water in the canals only, not directly on the soil. Do not water the canals if they have standing water in them or if the soil is very wet. Wait a day or two until the water has been absorbed into the soil, but don't let the soil dry out completely. It will take about 2 weeks for the seeds to germinate. Continue to

add water as needed, using the canals, and watch your seedlings grow. After about 6 weeks, you can plant the herbs outside in a garden.

The Maya believed that Chaak, the god of rain, brought the water needed to nourish the cornfields. They made sacrifices to Chaak so that he would continue to bring the rain. Another important god was Kinich Ahau, the sun god. The Maya believed that Kinich Ahau disappeared into the underworld each night at sunset. He turned into the jaguar god in the underworld, then returned each morning as the sun god.

WARRIORS

From historical records such as **codices** (ancient books), eyewitness accounts, and inscriptions on monuments, we know that the Maya were obsessed with war. This obsession came from their need to control more territory. They also needed to capture slaves and others for sacrifice. Capturing a rival leader was considered a great success and almost always sealed his fate as a sacrificial victim. Historians believe it is more likely that the Maya fought frequent small battles rather than full-scale destructive wars.

Brave Fighters

Warriors were part of the upper class, but the definition of warrior changed over time. In the early period of the Maya civilization, anyone who was needed to fight could be a warrior, including farmers, skilled laborers, and slaves. But as the civilization progressed, warriors became a specialized group of people who were trained to fight in battle. They wore fancy helmets, which were headdresses in the image of jaguars and birds. They often painted their bodies black and red before battle. Their attendants, the lower-ranking soldiers, carried brightly colored banners, beat drums, and blew trumpets and whistles. Warriors wore armor made of **tapir** (an animal found in tropical America) hides and quilted cotton, which was many layers of cotton sewn together, soaked in salt water, and then dried to form a stiff protective covering. They carried shields made of thick deer or jaguar hides.

Priests from both armies carried the image of their war god. Each army paid respect to the other's god before any fighting began. All fighting stopped at sundown so that men could eat food that women had prepared. Women accompanied men on these battles, but they went as cooks, not as fighters.

Although war happened frequently, it did not occur during farming season. Farming was more important than war. Wars usually took place after the harvest and until the next farming cycle began.

Weapons

Maya warriors fought with wooden clubs, flint knives, spears with flint points, axes, a three-pointed knife called a trident carved from a shell, and slingshots. Warriors were also known

UNPLEASANT DEATH

If a warrior captured an enemy leader, the captive was killed by being beheaded or by having his heart removed in a ritual sacrifice. Rival war leaders made the best captives of all, because the higher the rank of the sacrificial victim, the more the victors would be blessed by the gods.

to use hornet bombs; they would throw a hornet's nest into a group of enemy soldiers, and it would break open, releasing angry, stinging hornets. The Maya flung arrows, darts, and stones from slings. Maya weapons were made from bone and other parts of animals, stone, metal, and wood. Weaponry had little or no decoration.

Powerful Symbol

The Maya worshipped the jaguar, or *balam,* as it was called by the Maya. The jaguar is a powerful creature that symbolized strength and bravery to the Maya. The Maya considered the jaguar a protector of royalty and an intermediary between the living and the dead. To honor this animal, the Maya wore jaguar skin as clothing during wartime, festivals, and rituals; they captured the image of the jaguar on all types of works of art, including bowls, murals, vases, stone carvings, and headdresses; and they sat on jaguar-skin thrones. Maya warriors carried jaguar-skin shields during battle.

JAGUAR SHIELD

In this project, you will make a model of a Maya shield.

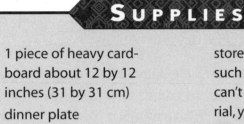

SUPPLIES

- 1 piece of heavy cardboard about 12 by 12 inches (31 by 31 cm)
- dinner plate
- pencil
- ruler
- scissors
- 72 inches (183 cm) of 1-inch (2.5-cm) wide ribbon, either with jaguar spots or a solid color
- ½ yard (.5 m) of fake leopardskin material (available at sewing stores, craft

stores, or discount stores, such as Wal-Mart). If you can't find the right material, you can always draw a jaguar pelt with markers. The background color of the pelt is a light tan and the spots are black.

- tape measure
- liquid craft glue
- 86 inches (218 cm) of rawhide lacing
- markers (optional)

STEPS

1 Lay the plate facedown on the cardboard. Trace the plate on the cardboard using the pencil. The diameter should be about 10½ inches (27 cm), but it doesn't have to be exact. Cut out the shape. This is your shield.

2 Cut pieces of material and ribbon to cover and decorate the shield.

3 Decorate the shield by gluing the pieces of ribbon and material to the front of the shield in an interesting design. Look at the finished shield shown here as an example. Let the glue dry completely.

4 *Note: Ask an adult for help.* Have an adult poke small holes 1 inch (2.5 cm) in from the edge of the shield and about 1½ inches (4 cm) apart with the tip of the scissors. You will be poking holes through both the material and the cardboard.

5 Cut a 50-inch (127-cm) piece of rawhide lacing and push one end up through any hole on the back of the shield. Pull it through the hole, leaving a 2-inch (5-cm) piece out the back. Bring the rawhide around the edge of the shield and push the rawhide up through the next hole on the back. Keep lacing the rawhide around the shield until you reach the hole you started with. Push the end of the rawhide out the back of the shield and tie the two ends together in a knot.

6 With the remaining material, cut three pieces that will be used for tails that are each about 2 by 8 inches (5 by 20 cm). Cut 3 pieces of rawhide lacing that are each about 6 inches (15 cm) long. Tie one end of each rawhide piece to a tail end, then attach the tails to the

shield by tying the other end of the rawhide to the rawhide that is threaded around the bottom of the shield. You can glue pieces of ribbon to the back of the shield, letting them hang down next to the tails.

7 To make a handle, cut a piece of rawhide lacing about 14 inches (36 cm) long. Tie one end to a piece of rawhide on the back top of the shield, and tie the other end to a piece of rawhide on the back bottom of the shield.

KINGS

Maya kings were absolute rulers and were believed to be descendants of the gods. Because of this, the Maya people believed that the kings had sacred powers and could contact the gods for guidance on when to conduct religious ceremonies or wage war. Maya kings were all-powerful and ruled all aspects of society, from food production to temple building. They made sure that artists depicted them in ways that made them appear prominent and powerful. Artists usually drew them in profile to show their flattened foreheads and in elaborate costumes to show their status and association with a certain **deity** (god). Their bodies were often painted and tattooed. A Maya ruler usually had one wife, and she was referred to as queen or lady.

Maya kings and queens and their children were assisted by hundreds of people. For a special occasion such as the birth of an heir, musicians and dancers were called upon to play music and dance, poets might recite a special poem for the newborn, scribes would write about the event, and artists might record the event in a painting or sculpture.

The Royal Palace

Some royal palaces were large single-storied structures that were covered in plaster, built on low platforms, and had from one to several open courtyards. However, some palaces, like the one archeologists found at Cancuén in present-day Guatemala, had 3 stories, 170 rooms, and 11 courtyards. Some palaces were built on top of pyramids. By doing this the royals could elevate themselves, which enhanced their status in society. They lived in the palaces, but never in the pyramids. Palace rooms included dressing and storage rooms for ceremonial dress and receiving rooms richly decorated with curtains and jaguar-skin cushions for important guests and ambassadors from other city-states. Royals conducted administrative and government business in palaces.

Royal Symbols

Royals often wore clothes made from jaguar skins to signify high rank, power, authority, and an association with the gods. Kings might also incorporate the jaguar name into their own names, to signify a very high status. For example, the eighth successor to the Tikal throne took the name Great Jaguar Paw. Other kings chose names such as Smoke-Jaguar, Jaguar Bird Peccary, and Shield-Jaguar.

Tropical bird feathers played a prominent role in clothing status, and the Maya decorated royal garments, headdresses, fans, and shields with feathers from different birds. An especially important bird, the quetzal, was considered sacred to the Maya. It had beautiful iridescent green and scarlet feathers, and its tail feathers were two feet long. Today this bird is nearly **extinct** (no longer existing) due to hunting and the destruction of its habitat.

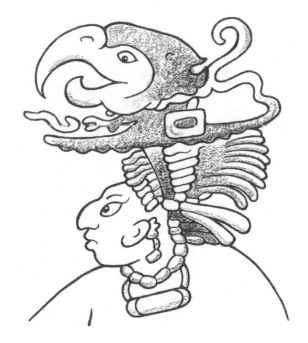

 MACAW HEADDRESS

Headdresses were an especially important symbol. The larger and more elaborate the headdress, the higher the status of the wearer. The Maya often fashioned the headdress in the shape of an animal's head, such as a jaguar or a bird. The image of a macaw, which represented the god called Celestial Bird, was used in a headdress worn by kings for special occasions. This deity was also known as Seven-Macaw and Serpent Bird and was associated with the four corners of the world.

Here's how you can make your own macaw headdress.

SUPPLIES

- 1 12-by-12-inch (31-by-31-cm) piece of oaktag
- pencil
- scissors
- transparent tape
- tape measure
- 1 large round balloon
- 1 package plaster cloth, available in craft and art supply stores
- masking tape
- medium-sized bowl
- acrylic craft paint in a variety of colors
- craft paintbrush
- 1 package brightly colored craft feathers, both rigid and soft
- liquid craft glue
- paper towels

STEPS

 1 Fold the oaktag in half. Draw a bird head with the top of the head on the fold of the oaktag as shown. The overall size will be about 5 inches (13 cm) long by 4 inches (10 cm) wide. Cut out the head through both thicknesses of oaktag, but don't cut *on* the fold—you want the two pieces to stay attached at the top of the head. Tape the beak together using the transparent tape. Set the head aside.

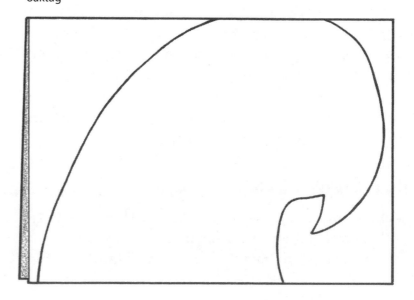

Draw top of head along fold.

Fold of oaktag

2 Have someone help you measure the **circumference** (distance around) of your head. Blow up the balloon to just slightly larger than that measurement and tie the end in a tight knot. Tape the knotted end of the balloon to your work surface using the masking tape.

3 Tape the neck of the bird head to the front top part of the balloon using the masking tape.

4 *Note: Check with an adult and read all of the plaster cloth directions before doing this step.* Cut the cloth into strips and fill the medium-sized bowl with warm water. Dipping one strip in the water at a time, start covering the top half of the balloon. (Note: It's good to gently shake off some of the excess water after dipping the strip.) Cover the entire oaktag bird head and beak with strips, smoothing the strips over the shape of the head.

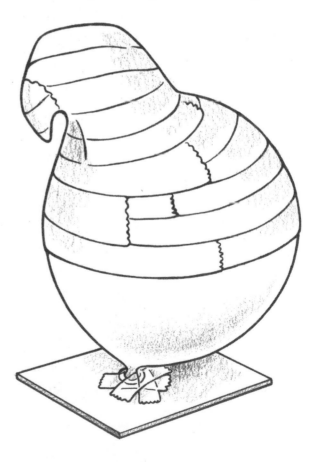

Continue applying strips to cover the top half of the balloon and the head until you have applied about 3 to 4 layers of the strips, smoothing them as you apply. *Note: Do not cover the bottom half of the balloon.*

5 Let the plaster cloth strips dry completely.

6 Pop the balloon and remove it from the plaster headdress. Paint the bird head so that it looks similar to the finished headdress.

7 While the paint is drying, start gluing on feathers, beginning at the bottom back of the head-dress. Keep a damp paper towel handy to wipe your fingers after you glue on each feather. To glue, squeeze a drop of glue on the headdress, place the end of the feather on the glue, then gently hold in place for a few seconds. The spines of the feathers will not adhere immediately. The feather part sticks better.

Put a drop of glue on body, then place feather on glue.

Overlap feathers so no white shows through.

However, once the glue has dried, the feathers should stay in place. Keep gluing on feathers until you cover the neck area and the back of the head. Use the rigid feathers for the wings and tail as shown.

8 Let the headdress dry completely before wearing it.

PART THREE

FOOD

The Maya diet was a plain and simple one that always included corn, beans, peppers, squash, and fruit such as mango, papaya, **cassava** (a tropical plant grown for its fleshy edible roots), and avocado. Stew, a meal containing a variety of foods cooked together, was a favorite. Maya women could make many different kinds of stews by combining some or all of the foods they grew, such as beans, corn, chili peppers, tomatoes, other vegetables, and seeds. Corn kernels ground into a paste thickened the liquid in the stew.

The average Maya did not eat meat on a regular basis, but when they did they enjoyed turkey, rabbit, armadillo, deer, duck, quail, and peccary, an animal similar to a pig. Fish, shellfish, snails, turtles, and sea birds were also eaten. The upper classes ate meat more frequently, though not every day. Meat was usually roasted over an open fire or made into a stew or soup with hot peppers and spices.

DOG FOOD

The Maya raised several breeds of dogs. Some were domesticated as pets. Others were fattened up for the family dinner table by being fed a diet rich in corn. The males were used for food, since the females were needed to give birth to puppies. A hairless breed of dog, similar in size to a pig, and a barkless breed were eaten. Some dogs were trained as hunting dogs, while others were sacrificed during ceremonies.

SACRED FOOD

Corn was the staple of the Maya diet. Corn made up 80 percent of the diet and was eaten as corn cakes, or tortillas, and in other forms, such as **tamales** (cornmeal dough rolled with a filling of ground meat or beans seasoned with chili, wrapped in corn husks, and steamed), corn balls or loaves eaten by workers as a snack, and corn porridge made from a kind of milk that was extracted from the ground maize and then drunk hot in the morning. Any leftover extracted milk that was not used up in the morning was saved, mixed with water, and drunk later in the day. Corn cakes were made twice a day and eaten at every meal. The Maya ate corn cakes as a bread, used them as a food scoop, or filled them with different foods, especially beans, squash, chili peppers, and sometimes meat.

Before any corn was planted, the farmer conducted a ceremony to honor the earth. The Maya believed corn was a miracle gift from the gods and called it "sunbeam of the gods."

Corn Preparation

First, corn kernels were removed from the cob. The Maya invented a simple tool that made this job easy. They used a deer bone or a piece of wood that had been sharpened to a point at one end. Women slid the pointed end of the tool down under a row of kernels, which separated the kernels from the cob. They repeated this for each row until all the kernels had been removed.

Next, women set out the kernels to dry so they could be stored for later use. When they needed to prepare the corn, they then soaked the dried kernels in a water-and-lime mixture, or if lime wasn't available, they used ground seashells.

DISEASE FIGHTER

Lime (calcium oxide), which comes from limestone or ground seashells, was a necessary part of the corn preparation process because calcium oxide makes it possible for the body to absorb the niacin in the grain. Niacin, part of the B complex vitamin, prevents the vitamin deficiency pellagra, which causes a person's skin to peel. No one knows how the Maya learned about this, but they must have accidentally discovered the health benefits of using lime.

THE CORN GOD

The Maya corn god was called Yum K'aax. He was pictured as a young man with hair of corn silk and a corn head-dress. Researchers speculate that this god may have been seen as needing the farmer's help to survive. The farmers chased the birds and insects away from the corn and performed ceremonies to the rain god, Chaak, to bring water to the corn plants.

Once the kernels had soaked sufficiently, the women ground them on a stone slab made from **basalt** (a volcanic stone) using a cylindrical stone as a rolling pin. This grinding process turned the kernels into a thick dough called *zacan* from which the women made tortillas.

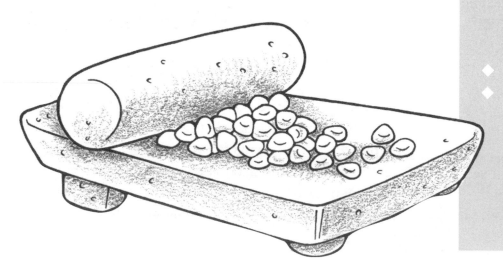

ANCIENT TEFLON

Maya women made their own cookware with a special nonstick surface. First they made a large, flat dish from clay. Then they rubbed the surface with a layer of fine clay mixed with ground talc and water. After the dish dried, the women polished the entire surface with a smooth stone. This created a nonstick surface that was great for cooking flat corn cakes.

CORN CAKES

In this activity, you'll make your own corn cakes and a simple salsa to go with them.

INGREDIENTS

MAKES 16 CORN CAKES

◆ 2 cups (.5 l) instant masa harina* (also called masa)

◆ 1⅛ cups (266 ml) lukewarm water

*A kind of corn flour found in Mexican/Hispanic food stores, many supermarkets, or on-line (see page x for Web sites). The King Arthur Flour baker's catalogue sells it by mail. Call 1-800-827-6836 for more information. If you use regular masa instead of instant, follow the directions on the package.

U T E N S I L S

- measuring cup
- medium-sized mixing bowl
- mixing spoon
- paper towels
- plastic wrap

- cast-iron skillet or frying pan
- rolling pin
- spatula
- dinner plate
- clean dish towel

S T E P S

1 In the bowl, mix together the instant masa harina and lukewarm water until thoroughly combined. Place dough on a clean surface and knead until pliable and smooth, about 5 minutes. If dough is too sticky, add a bit more masa harina; if it begins to dry and crack, sprinkle with a little water.

2 Divide the dough into 16 equal-sized balls. Remove one ball and place it on a clean surface. Cover the rest of the dough balls with a few damp paper towels.

3 *Ask an adult for help with using the stove.* Preheat the cast-iron skillet or frying pan to medium.

4 Place the ball you removed from the bowl between two sheets of plastic wrap and press the dough flat using a rolling pin or your hands. Continue to flatten evenly until the dough is slightly thinner than a pie crust.

5 Immediately place the tortilla on the preheated pan and allow the bottom of the tortilla to cook for approximately 30 seconds. Use the spatula to turn the tortilla over to cook for approximately 30 seconds more, then transfer to a plate. Cover the cooked tortillas with the clean dish towel. Repeat this process with each ball of dough. Keep the cooked tortillas covered with the towel so that they stay warm and moist until ready to serve.

Now that you've made your tortillas, here's a simple recipe for a salsa you can scoop up with your tortillas.

XNI PEC

(*Xni pec* is the name the ancient Maya used for tomato-and-chili salsa)

INGREDIENTS

- 2 medium tomatoes
- ½ small yellow onion
- 14.25-ounce (120-g) jar or can of mild diced green chilies
- ½ orange
- ½ lime
- salt to taste

UTENSILS

- cutting board
- knife
  Note: Adult help needed when using knife
- medium-sized mixing bowl
- mesh strainer
- small bowl
- mixing spoon

STEPS

1 Chop the tomatoes into small chunks and discard the stem area. Place the chopped tomatoes in the bowl.

2 Cut the onion in half, peel one half, and put the other half in the refrigerator. Chop the peeled half into small pieces. Place it in the bowl with the tomato chunks. Use the strainer to drain the liquid from the chilies, then add the chilies to the tomato chunks.

3 Cut the orange in half and squeeze the juice from one half into the small bowl. Remove any seeds that fall into the bowl. You can eat the other half or put it in the refrigerator.

4 Cut the lime in half and squeeze the juice from one half into the small bowl with the orange juice. Remove any seeds that fall into the bowl. Put the other half in the refrigerator. Stir with the mixing spoon. Pour the juice into the bowl with the chopped tomatoes, onions, and chilies.

5 Mix all ingredients together. Serve with tortillas.

FIRE FOOD

The Maya ate chili peppers daily, mainly as a spice to add more flavor to the dishes they prepared. Some varieties of chili peppers were extremely hot, while others tasted mild. The Maya used the mild-tasting chilies as a fresh vegetable. Many of the hot chilies were dried and used as spices. There are pictures in Maya codices showing men and gods breathing fire after eating hot chili peppers.

To grind both dried and fresh chili peppers, the ancient Maya used special pottery. The inside of the bowl had a rough surface of ridges that helped make the grinding easier. Many Maya today continue to use this traditional bowl for grinding chili peppers, but others use a mortar and pestle. A mortar is a bowl and a pestle is a sticklike object with a rounded tip. Cooks place dried chili peppers or other herbs in the mortar and use the pestle to grind the dried ingredients. The mortar and pestle are usually made from marble, porcelain, hardwood, or stoneware.

HEALING QUALITIES

The Maya discovered uses for chili peppers other than just as a food. They also used chili peppers to make medicine. When a person had a wound, a Maya doctor would spread mashed roasted chili peppers mixed with honey over the wound. This helped stop any infection. A chili tea helped people get rid of headaches, earaches, chest congestion, and intestinal problems.

Many people today continue to use chili peppers for health reasons. Capsaicin, a compound found in chili peppers, is believed to help lower cholesterol and clear sinus congestion. It has helped people with digestive problems and has been used to stop bleeding. If put in an ointment, it can lessen the pain from arthritis, which is an inflammation of the joints in the body.

CHICKEN CHILI PACAL

STEPS

Safety Alert! Be careful when handling raw chicken. Salmonella and other bacteria that make people sick may be found in uncooked chicken. This bacteria is killed when chicken is thoroughly cooked. Always wash your hands thoroughly with soap and hot water after handling raw chicken. Never place raw chicken on a counter. Always use a plastic cutting board for chicken. Clean all utensils and cutting boards in the dishwasher or in plenty of hot water and soap.

1 Place the sliced onion, the sliced chilies, the sliced red pepper, and the chopped cilantro in one of the large bowls.

2 Place the 2 tablespoons (29 ml) of olive oil, the juice from the orange and lemon, and the chicken broth in the other large bowl.

3 Stir the olive oil, the juices, and the chicken broth together well. Pour most of the liquid over the sliced vegetables. Leave some liquid in the bowl and place the chicken breasts in this bowl. Turn the chicken to coat both sides with the liquid.

INGREDIENTS

SERVINGS: 4

- 1 small yellow onion, peeled and cut into slices
- 2 fresh chili peppers, cut into slices, stems and seeds removed. (Choose from poblano, Anaheim, or cubanelle. Choose one type or mix two together.) *Safety Alert! Although these chili peppers are mild, always keep fingers away from your eyes and face when handling fresh chili peppers. Wash your hands in hot water and soap after handling the peppers.*
- 1 red bell pepper, cut into slices, stem and seeds removed
- 1 teaspoon (5 ml) chopped fresh cilantro
- 3 tablespoons (30 ml) olive oil
- 1 orange
- 1 lemon
- ½ cup (118 ml) chicken broth
- 1 pound (450 gr) boneless chicken breast
- salt and pepper to taste

UTENSILS

- knife
  Note: Adult help needed when using knife.
- plastic cutting board
- 2 large bowls
- mixing spoon
- medium-sized frying pan
- measuring spoons
- small saucepan
- serving platter

4 Sprinkle the sliced vegetables and the chicken breasts with salt and pepper and mix well. Set both bowls in the refrigerator.

5 The chicken will **marinate** (steep in a liquid to enhance flavor) in the refrigerator for about 10 minutes.

6 When the chicken has finished marinating, heat the frying pan to medium high for a few minutes, then add 1 tablespoon (14 ml) of olive oil to the pan. Remove the chicken from the refrigerator and place the chicken breasts in the pan. *(Note: Throw out the marinade from this bowl.)* Sauté the chicken over medium to medium-high heat for about 10 minutes or until it is completely cooked, turning the chicken breasts over once during cooking. They should be nicely browned.

7 While the chicken is cooking, put the vegetable/liquid mixture from the other bowl into the medium saucepan and heat it over medium-high heat for about 10 to 15 minutes, stirring occasionally.

COOKING WITH STONES

The early Maya made pottery, but they did not use it for cooking. Instead, they cooked food in tightly woven, waterproofed baskets. They filled the baskets with water and food, then placed heated stones in the basket. The heat cooked the food.

8 When the chicken is cooked, place it on the platter and pour the warm vegetable mixture over it. Serve immediately with rice and tortillas.

FOOD OF THE GODS

The Maya cultivated a tree that produced cacao beans. These beans, highly valued by the Maya, were used as a kind of money as well as for food. One favorite use for the cacao bean was to make a chocolate drink enjoyed by the upper-class Maya. First the beans were crushed, then they were ground into a fine powder. The person making the drink placed the powder and water in a decorative vessel with a spout and stirred the mixture. Once the powder had dissolved, the person held the vessel above his or her head and poured the drink into another vessel on the ground. This process was repeated until the drink became foamy. That was how the Maya enjoyed the beverage most. Sometimes they added honey, vanilla, and chili peppers to add flavor. They also liked the drink served hot.

Here's an easy recipe for a chocolate drink that is similar to the one enjoyed by the ancient Maya. The original recipe contained a variety of chili peppers, which made the drink quite spicy. Note: Two of the optional ingredients in this recipe are ground chili peppers. These spices are rated according to "hotness." Mild is not very hot and medium is a bit hotter.

CHILI CHOCOLATE DRINK

(*Chilcacahuatl*)

INGREDIENTS

SERVINGS: 3

- 3 cups (.75 l) water
- 2 teaspoons (10 ml) mild ground chili ancho* (optional)
- ¼ teaspoon (1 ml) medium chili chipotle* (optional)
- ½ teaspoon (2.5 ml) ground allspice
- 1 tablespoon (15 ml) vanilla powder
- ½ cup (118 ml) unsweetened cocoa powder
- ½ cup (118 ml) honey

*Many supermarkets carry these spices. You can also find them in Mexican/Hispanic grocery stores or online (see page x for Web sites).

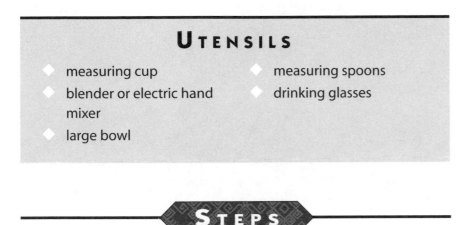

UTENSILS

- measuring cup
- blender or electric hand mixer
- large bowl
- measuring spoons
- drinking glasses

STEPS

1 Measure and pour the water into the blender, or if you don't have a blender, the large bowl.

2 Measure the spices one at a time, and place in the blender or bowl of water.

3 Measure and pour the cocoa powder and honey into the blender or bowl.

4 Mix well in the blender or with the electric mixer so that all ingredients are blended. Pour into the glasses and serve. (Note: If you don't like the medium "hotness" of the ground chipotle, you can leave it out.)

PART FOUR

ART AND ARCHITECTURE

Maya artists were an educated, creative group of people who belonged to the upper class. Artists created beautiful sculptures, masks, murals, pottery, jewelry, and elaborate headdresses in a variety of media, including stone, wood, paint, plaster, shell, and jade. To decorate a piece, the artist could use paint in a wide array of colors, use a combination of carving and painting, stamp the object with dye or paint, or add precious gems or exotic feathers to the object. Maya artists used "slip paint," a mixture of ground **pigment** (a powdered substance mixed with liquid used to color other materials), clay, and water, to decorate their pottery and other objects. Vivid blues, greens, reds, oranges, and browns were used in murals, though most of the paints have faded or disintegrated over time. Maya painters used seashells as paint pots and animal hair for brushes. Painted decorations included images of myths, rituals, geometric designs, and hieroglyphs. No matter how small the decoration, it was never used solely for decorative purposes but always had a specific meaning.

To honor Maya royalty, artists created **stelae** (standing stone columns). Carved into these stone columns were hieroglyphic texts that gave information about the ruler. It might include his birth date, marriage information, coronation date, and important battles. The stelae were erected in the plazas of each city-state. Some stelae were more than 30 feet (10 m) high. The oldest Maya stele dates back to 328 B.C. and was found in the city of Uaxactún, the oldest of the Maya cities.

Maya architects worked with engineers to design the great buildings in their cities. Engineers made sure that the city had a drainage system, **aqueducts** (channels for water), bridges, roads, and **causeways** (raised surfaces across wet ground or water). Architects mapped out the city with careful consideration for the placement of temple-pyramids, courtyards, public squares, palaces, and other monuments, and they kept a close watch over building projects once they began. Maya cities often had a similar layout with buildings arranged around open plazas. While the Maya architects didn't originate many of the building designs they used (the Olmecs, for example, built pyramids a thousand years before the Maya), they did refine the art of building and made their structures more complex and sophisticated.

The Maya excelled in the art of creating impressive buildings of stone, all without the use of metal tools. They were constantly building larger structures over older buildings. The outside surfaces of many buildings were decorated with giant stone or stucco masks or images of the gods or kings. Some stone buildings were built to observe the stars and planets.

CORBEL ARCH

One of the Maya's unique contributions to architecture is the corbel arch, also called the Maya arch, which was formed by projecting stone blocks out from each side of a wall until they almost met, forming a peak. A row of stone blocks at the top of the peak served as a bridge for the space between the two sides of the arch. Because of this space at the top, the corbel arch is not considered a true arch, which the Maya never mastered. The corbel arch is also weaker than a true arch.

In contrast, the ancient Romans mastered the arch design by placing a keystone block in the space at the top of the peak. This helped distribute the force of the upper blocks to the side columns of the arch, making this a much stronger structure.

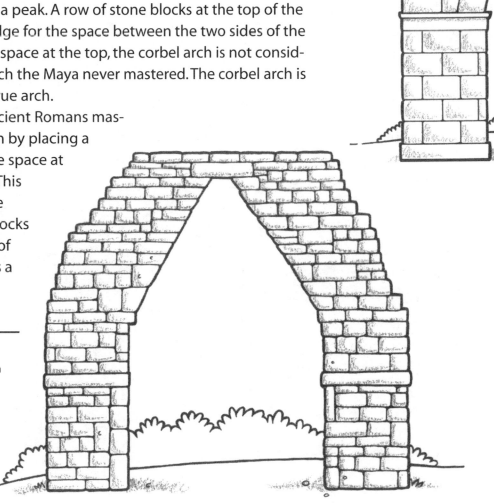

Maya arch

Roman arch

WEAVING

According to a Maya legend, the goddess of weaving, Ix Chebel Yax, taught a Maya woman to weave by showing her a spider weaving a web. Maya women from all social classes practiced the art of weaving, and the Maya wove everything from clothes and tapestries to tablecloths and napkins. Young slave girls aspired to be great weavers. If they excelled at this art, they would not be considered for sacrifice.

The Backstrap Loom

The backstrap loom is a weaving device that has been used in Mesoamerica since around 1500 B.C. It is also called the hip loom and the stick loom. Because of its portability, Maya women could weave anywhere. In the backstrap loom, a group of threads, the warp, are attached to a stick that is fastened to a fixed object, such as a tree. The other ends of these threads are then attached to another stick that is fastened to a belt worn around the woman's lower back. The woman could then stretch the threads tight during weaving by moving her body away from the tree. Threads called weft threads were woven in between the warp threads to create the design. Cloth woven on a backstrap loom is generally no more than about 2 feet (60 cm) wide. But this did not pose a problem for Maya weavers. They would sew strips of cloth together to make wider cloth for garments.

NATURAL DYES

The Maya created their own dyes from nature. They produced a wide array of colors from a few items. To create a colorful range from pink to red to purple, the Maya used the **cochineal** (a tiny red insect that lives in the prickly pear). Snails produced the color purple, and the indigo plant made many shades of blue. The Maya also used minerals to create dyes.

Ancient Designs

The designs or combinations of designs the Maya chose as decorations for their textiles were often based on mythology and symbolism. Even the simplest of designs contained a complex message. Animals such as the jaguar, snake, deer, and monkey, which played an important part in Maya mythology, were often part of the design. Other important symbols were the cornstalk and the *Yaxche*, the Maya Tree of Life. Historians have identified hundreds of designs from ancient Maya textiles. Maya weavers rarely used the same design twice. Today, Maya weavers keep this art alive by continuing to use these ancient designs. Locals can identify the village of the wearer by the specific design woven into the cloth.

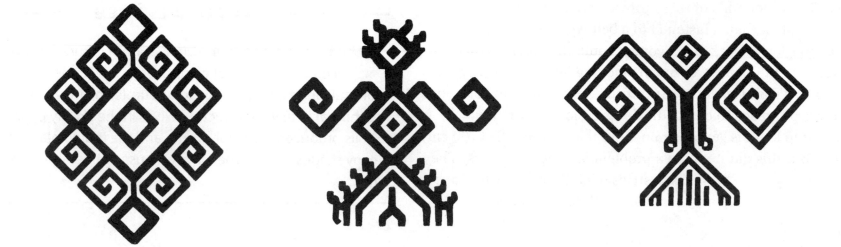

WOVEN WALL HANGING

You can make a simple, colorful woven wall hanging in the style of the Maya weavers.

SUPPLIES

- pencil
- ruler
- piece of heavy cardboard
- scissors

- 1 package of 100 percent cotton embroidery floss in bright colors
- 1 embroidery needle with blunt tip
- clean hair comb

STEPS

1 Draw a 7-by-4¼-inch (18-by-11-cm) rectangle on the heavy cardboard and cut it out. Along each short edge of the rectangle, make 16 pencil marks ¼ inch (.5 cm) apart, then cut on the marks to make slits about ¼ inch (.5 cm) deep. This is your loom.

2 Cut a piece of cotton floss in any color about 8 yards (7 m) long. This is the **warp** (the stationary strands on a loom). Place the warp on the loom by putting it through the bottom left slit, leaving an 8-inch (20-cm) tail out the back of the loom. Wrap the floss around the loom, working from bottom to top and left to right through each slit in turn. When you reach the top right slit, leave an 8-inch (20-cm) tail out the back of the loom. Turn the loom over, facedown, and tie the two tails together in a tight knot.

3 Cut a piece of floss in any color about 84 inches (213 cm) long and thread it on the needle. This is the **weft** (the strands that are woven into the warp).

4 Turn the loom faceup and start weaving at the bottom right of the loom by placing the needle *under* the first warp, then *over* the next warp, *under* the next, and so on until you reach the left side of the loom. Gently pull the weft all the way through, leaving a 4-inch (10-cm) tail on the right. For the second row, weave back toward the right side of the loom, placing the needle *under* the first left warp, *over* the next warp, and so on until you reach the right side. Pull the weft gently, making sure the left and right sides of the warp don't pull in. Use the comb to pack, or push down, each row close to the previous one. *Do this each time you weave a row.*

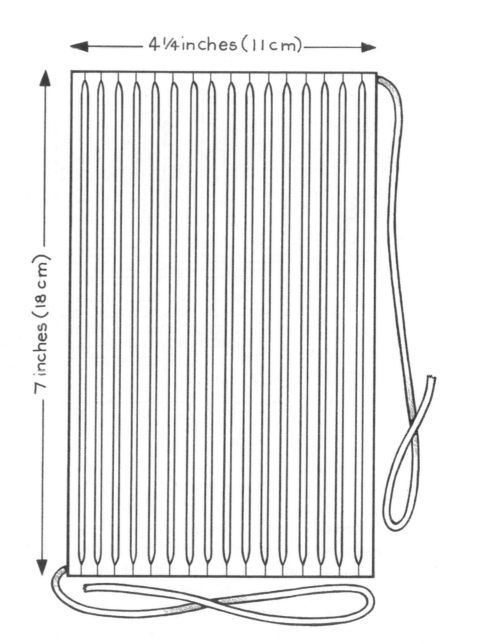

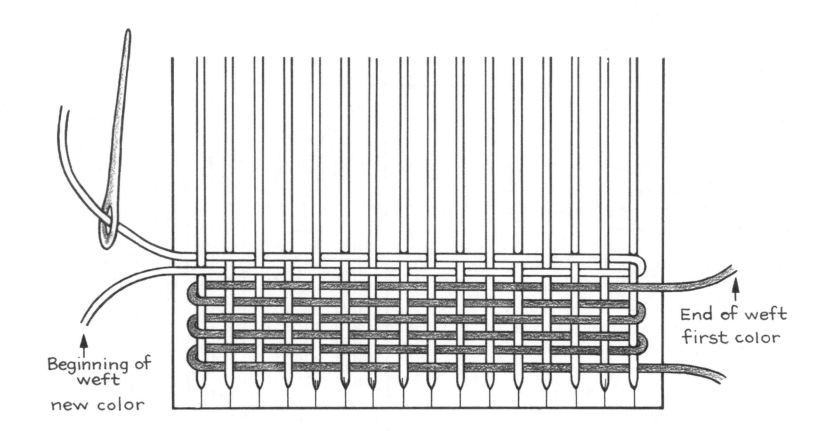

Beginning of
weft
new color

End of weft
first color

5 Now be creative. Continue weaving, using many different colors to create narrow rows or fewer colors to create wider rows. Or weave a combination of the two. Alternate colors to create a pattern if you'd like. When you need a new color, start weaving the new color on the opposite side of where you just ended. Remember to weave the new row opposite to the way you wove the previous row. Do not cut the floss ends sticking out. You will cut these later. Make sure the floss ends are about 2 inches (5 cm) long.

6 Remember to pack each row tightly. Continue weaving until you reach the top and can't weave another row. Turn the loom facedown and cut across the

middle of the unwoven warp , cutting through the two knotted strands.

7 Turn the loom faceup and remove the warp strands from the slits along the bottom of the cardboard. Tie the first two warp strands on the bottom left together in a tight knot close to the edge of the weaving. Tie the next pair of strands together, and repeat until all pairs are tied.

8 Repeat Step 7 for the warp strands on the top of the weaving.

9 Trim the warp strands to a length of about $^1/_2$ inch (1 cm).

10 Carefully trim the floss ends from the weft that are sticking out of the rows.

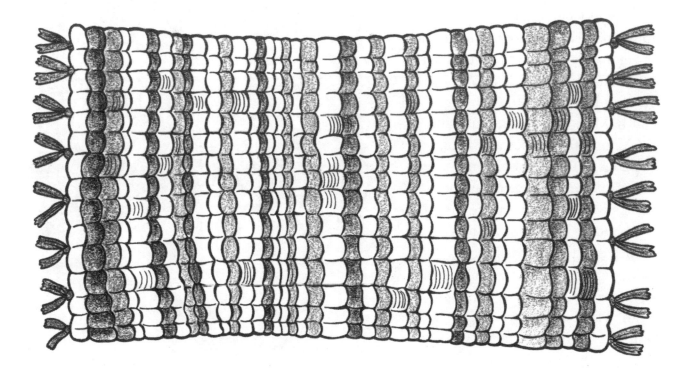

MASK MAKING

The Maya used many different kinds of masks for various ceremonies. They used materials such as stone, obsidian, gold, wood, stucco, shell, and jade, or a combination of these materials, to create the masks. Special artists made these masks for religious rituals, celebrations, festivals, and for rulers to wear after death. Masks for ceremonies and festivals took the shapes and images of the gods, animals, or a combination of both. The Maya wearing the masks would pretend to be these gods and goddesses or animals. Some ceremonial masks were made by attaching jade pieces and other semiprecious stones to a human skull. These masks were also used in temples as offerings to the gods.

The Maya, like other civilizations, created death masks for their rulers to wear after death. The death mask, which portrayed the king's face, was both a protection from the dangers in the afterlife and a way to keep the king's image alive. The wealthiest city-states sometimes buried their rulers with jade masks.

Mask Decoration

Masks ran the gamut from simple stone images of a ruler to elaborate works of art decorated with precious gems, feathers, textiles, and human hair. Some of the most beautiful masks for rulers to use in ceremonies were **inlaid** (decorated with a pattern set into the surface) with pieces of cut gems to create a **mosaic** (a decoration made by placing small pieces of different-colored material on a surface to form a pattern). These masks could contain hundreds of cut gem pieces. Masks worn by people in the lower ranks of the upper class might be simply carved from wood.

Lord Pacal's Mask

Lord Pacal, the ruler of the Maya city of Palenque, was one of the most powerful of the Maya rulers. It is said that Lord Pacal played a key role in inspiring artists to create beautiful works of art and architects to design splendid buildings. Pacal came to power at the age of 12 and lived to be 80 years old.

A Mexican archeologist, Dr. Alberto Ruz Lhuillier, and his team discovered the **sarcophagus** (stone coffin) of Lord Pacal in 1952. The lid was carved with the most elaborate artwork

and hieroglyphs anyone had ever seen. It depicts Lord Pacal at the moment of his death, falling into the underworld. He was buried wearing jade rings on all his fingers, and a stone sculpture of his head was found in his coffin. His death mask, found inside the sarcophagus, was a mosaic mask made of pieces of jade, shell, and obsidian.

SPECIAL JADE

For very special masks, the Maya used apple green jade, a gem they highly prized. They called it the stone of grace. It was a very hard jade, one of the hardest, called jadeite, collected from riverbeds. To cut through its hard surface, the Maya invented a type of drill made from a stick with a pointed end of obsidian. They would sprinkle the surface of the jade with quartz sand, then spin the drill on the quartz. The friction created by the drill bit, or tip of the drill, and the quartz sand cut the jade.

MOSAIC MASK

Follow these directions to make your own replica of Lord Pacal's mosaic mask.

SUPPLIES

- 1 friend
- 1 package of plaster cloth, available at craft or art supply stores
- scissors
- old towel
- hair clip
- petroleum jelly
- medium-sized bowl of water

- craft acrylic paint, gold
- craft paintbrush
- small bowl of water
- paper towels
- 3 sheets of green construction paper, 8½ by 11 inches (22 by 28 cm)
- liquid craft glue
- white scrap paper (optional)

STEPS

1 *Note: Have an adult help you with this project. Read all of the directions on the plaster cloth package before starting this project!* Do not do this project alone.

2 Cut the plaster cloth into strips before you begin. The strips will be different sizes depending on where you use them on your face, but start with strips that measure 5 by 2 inches (13 by 5 cm). Then cut some smaller ones that measure 1 by 3 inches (2.5 by 8 cm). Set the strips aside.

3 Wrap your hair in the towel and use the hair clip to hold the towel in place. The towel will help keep your hair away from your face.

4 *Smear a thin layer of petroleum jelly over your entire face, including your eyebrows. You do not need to put any on your eyelids or lips. Do not skip this step.*

5 Have a friend dip the plaster strips into the bowl of water one at a time, gently shake off excess water, and apply the strips to your face, being careful *not* to

cover your eyes, nostrils, or mouth. Here are some tips for applying the strips: Start at the top of the face and work your way down. Make sure the strips overlap, and press them gently to conform to the shape of the face. You can apply three to four layers of strips.

6 After your friend has applied the strips, have him or her carefully remove the mask from your face and set it aside to dry completely. Wipe the petroleum jelly off your face with a paper towel. Then wash your face with soap and water.

7 Paint the mask gold and let it dry completely.

8 While the paint is drying, cut pieces of the green construction paper. They do not have to be the same size. However, the pieces should not be larger than 1 by 1½ inches (2.5 by 4 cm). If you look at Lord Pacal's mask, you'll notice that the jade pieces are different shapes and sizes. Cut enough to cover your mask.

9 Squeeze some glue on the back of a cut piece of construction paper and gently press it in place at the top of the mask. Continue to glue pieces to the mask one at a time. Do not let all sides of the pieces touch. Leave a tiny space between *some* of the pieces so that the gold paint shows through.

1. Apply a thin layer of petroleum jelly over entire face. Do not get any in your eyes.
2. Apply strips over face. Avoid eyes, lips, and nostrils.

Glue different-size "mosaic pieces" over entire surface of painted mask.

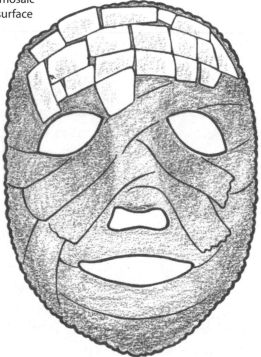

11 This step is optional. From the white scrap paper, cut two ovals for the eyes, color in a black circle for the eye on each piece, then glue these pieces to the inside of the mask, eyeballs facing out.

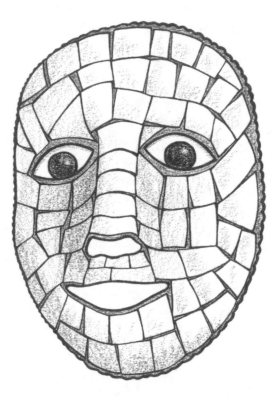

10 Continue working until the entire mask is covered with the green "mosaic" pieces. You may need to recut pieces of the construction paper to fit a certain spot on the mask. Let the mask dry completely.

POTTERY

Maya potters created highly sophisticated pieces of art, such as **incense burners** (containers for a material that when burned produces a fragrant odor), bowls, vases, plates, statues, and many other objects. Pottery pieces were often either painted or sculpted with the heads of gods. The more elaborate pieces were used for rituals or made for the rich. People in the lower classes used simpler pieces with little decoration. Maya potters didn't use a potter's wheel. Everything they made was shaped with their hands. Maya potters **fired** (heated in an oven called a kiln) their pieces at very low temperatures. This made for pottery that was beautiful but less durable than pots fired at higher temperatures.

Many of the vases created by the Maya potters were cylindrical. This type of vase usually contained hieroglyphic texts on the outside that described the purpose of the vase. For example, one vase was used to store cacao while another stored a mixture of cacao and fruit seeds. Many of these vases were given as gifts to the elite members of society. Archeologists have found some pieces that show no wear at all, while others show a great deal of use.

Assembly-Line Pottery

Though Maya artists created most pottery by hand, they sometimes made small clay figurines using a mold. The mold was carved in the image of a figure, such as a god, a king, a warrior, or other person of importance. When clay was pressed into the mold, the image of the figure was imprinted into the clay. These figurines could be produced quickly and cheaply, so they were probably meant for the average Maya instead of for royalty.

MAYA BLUE

The Maya who lived in Sakalum, in the northern part of the empire, created an incredibly brilliant blue durable pigment. To achieve this color, the artist mixed **indigo** (a blue dye obtained from plants) with a clay that was dug from the edges of the cenotes and that was found only in that area. This mixture could be ground into a substance that could be mixed with water and used as a paint or dye for pottery, murals, sculptures, and figurines. Today researchers are analyzing this substance to learn the secret of its durability.

PAINTED VASE

After the potter had shaped the clay vase and let it dry, the potter covered it with a layer of **stucco** (a durable finish for exterior or interior walls usually made of cement, sand, and lime) and then painted on a design before the stucco dried. This method, called **fresco** (the art of painting on moist lime plaster with water-based pigments), enabled the paint to dry into the surface of the stucco, making it last longer. Painted vases were used in religious ceremonies, for sacrificial offerings, and as decorative pieces. The painted scenes on vases might depict rulers, rituals, gods, animals, or events that took place in the underworld, and they often contained writing.

You can sculpt a clay vase with painted images similar to an ancient Maya vase.

SUPPLIES

- self- or water-hardening craft clay
- small bowl of water
- ruler
- craft acrylic paints in a variety of colors
- craft paintbrush
- paper towels

STEPS

1 *(Note: Keep your fingers moist when working with clay.)* Flatten a piece of clay into a disk shape with a diameter of 4 inches (10 cm) and a thickness of about ½ inch (1 cm). Turn up the disk-shaped edge to begin forming the sides of the vase. If the turned-up edge overlaps, just pinch the overlapped parts together. The diameter of the bottom of the vase will now be about 3 inches (7.5 cm).

2 Make about 8 to 10 clay coils that measure about 9 inches (23 cm) long. Place one on the top edge of the base. Gently blend the coil and edge of the base together. Keep building the sides of the vase with coils until the vase measures about 4 inches (10 cm) high. Blend each coil so the outside and inside surfaces of the vase are smooth.

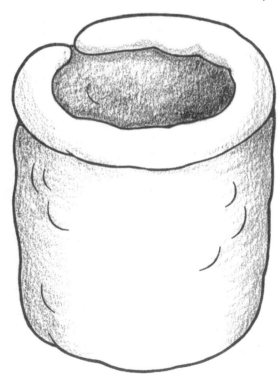

Attach clay coil, then smooth into body of vase.

3 Use the fresco method and paint your vase before the clay hardens. Paint the outside of the vase any color you like. Let the paint dry. Then paint on ancient Maya designs and glyphs before the clay hardens. (For designs and glyphs, see page 95.) When finished, allow the paint to dry and the clay to harden according to the directions that came with your clay. *Do not use this vase with water! It is only for decoration.*

BUILDING

Of all the ancient Maya buildings, the temple-pyramids remain one of the Maya's most impressive architectural achievements. These massive stone structures, constructed in the heart of Maya cities, towered from 155 to 288 feet (47 to 88 m) above the land. The city of Tikal alone had five enormous temple-pyramids. At the tops of the pyramids, the Maya erected temples where priests communicated with the gods.

The basic construction consisted of a central core of rocks and dirt at the base of the pyramid surrounded by a retaining wall. Platforms were built, one on top of the other, on this base. Each new added platform decreased in size, giving the pyramid a stepped look. Workers covered the outside surface of the pyramid with a thick layer of stucco. Certain workers were responsible for smoothing the stucco while others would paint the smoothed surface once it had hardened and dried. Historical evidence shows that red, along with other bright colors, was

Maya temple-pyramid

often used to paint the temple-pyramids. Experts believe that to the Maya, the color red meant renewal or rebirth because the Maya associated this color with the east or rising sun.

Burial chambers for royalty were built in the lower platforms. Some high rulers were cremated. This may have been done in areas where the limestone was hard to dig through. Their ashes were placed in urns and buried beneath temples. Some pyramids at Palenque had narrow shafts that ran from the king's tomb at the bottom to the top of the pyramid. The Maya believed these shafts made it easier for the dead king to communicate with the gods. In the early days, rulers' heads were mummified, kept in a family chapel, and "fed" regularly with food offerings.

ANCIENT BELIEF

The Maya built their temple-pyramids to resemble mountains. They did this because they believed that mountains housed their ancestors' souls. Today, the Maya continue to hold this belief.

No Easy Task!

Constructing a temple-pyramid was a difficult job. It required the efforts of many people, both workers and slaves. Before a pyramid could be constructed, the land had to be cleared of trees and shrubs, then leveled to make a surface that would support the foundation of the pyramid. Large slabs of stone had to be quarried from stone pits. Workers then had to move the stone slabs from the quarry to the construction site either by hand or by placing the slabs on log rollers. Since the Maya had no pack animals to pull these rollers, workers did all of this strenuous labor. At the site, **masons** (workers who build with brick or stone) would cut the stone into the shapes needed for the pyramids. The specific region where the pyramid was built determined the type of stone used. For example, limestone was popular in the lowlands, while sandstone was more available in the highlands.

Getting to the Top

Some temple-pyramids were tall with narrow sides, such as those at Tikal in the Petén rain forest. Others, such as those in Chichén Itzá, were wider and shorter. In both cases, however, the steps of the temple-pyramids were steep and the **treads** (horizontal surface area of the steps) were so narrow, that it was impossible to place the entire foot on the step's surface—a person had to walk up the steps with his or her feet facing sideways. Only priests and kings were allowed to walk to the top, and, dressed in their royal clothing, this careful placement of the feet made for a slower and more strenuous climb to the top. Experts believe that this was done to make reaching the top more rewarding.

The Temple of the Giant Jaguar

The great city of Tikal, located in the northern Petén, is considered to be one of the most spectacular cities of the Maya civilization. Historians believe that as many as 80,000 to 100,000 people may have lived in Tikal during the eighth and ninth centuries. Tikal was a huge complex of monuments and temple-pyramids. One of the most impressive structures in Tikal is the Temple of the Giant Jaguar. Yax Kin directed the construction of this pyramid, which was built around A.D. 700, as a sacred tomb for his father, Ah Cacau, Tikal's 26th king. This temple towers 145 feet (44 m) above the plaza and consists of nine steeply sloped platforms.

TEMPLE-PYRAMID

You can construct a replica of the Temple of the Giant Jaguar using clay, but your temple-pyramid will have fewer platforms.

STEPS

1 You will need 4 squares of clay, each decreasing in size by 1 inch (2.5 cm). Starting with a base piece that is 5 inches (13 cm) square, the piece after that should be 4 inches (10 cm) square, then 3 inches (7.5 cm) square, and finally 2 inches (5 cm) square. All of the squares should be ¾ to 1 inch (2 to 2.5 cm) thick.

2 Place the base square on your work surface. Drizzle glue on the top surface of the 5-inch square, then place the 4-inch square on top of the 5-inch square, so that it is evenly centered. Gently press this square in place. Repeat this step for the 3-inch square and the 2-inch square, until all squares are stacked in place.

Glue each square to the previous one before stacking.

3 Make sure the dowel is not longer than the height of the stacked squares. Gently push the dowel down through the center of the top square until it goes through all squares and reaches the bottom. Rub some clay over the end of the dowel at the top square to cover it.

4 To make the stairway, form a solid triangle from clay that has a 90° angle, a height of about 3 to 4 inches (8 to 10 cm). The triangle should not be taller than the height of the stacked squares. Don't make the overall triangle too thick, although the base of the triangle will be thicker than the top. The base should measure about 1 inch long by ¹/₂ inch thick (2.5 by 1 cm).

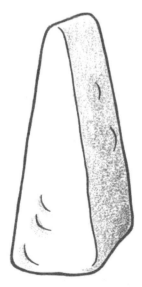

5 Gently press the solid triangle shape to the center of the front of the pyramid. You will need to angle the stairway back so it rests against the angle of the pyramid. Use your fingers to smooth the edges where the stair piece is attached to the pyramid. To make the steps, use the molding tool to make horizontal slits from the base of the stairs to the top, using your fingers to mold the stairs as needed.

6 Look at the picture of the Temple of the Giant Jaguar on page 81. Mold a small top piece for the pyramid similar to the one in the picture. Glue it in place on the very top of your pyramid. Place the pyramid on the rack. Let the pyramid dry according to the directions that came with the clay.

7 Paint the pyramid red as the Maya did, or choose any color you like. Let the paint dry completely. If you use different colors, clean the paintbrush in the small bowl of water. Dry the brush on the paper towel before using another color. (Note: It's best to put your pyramid on your desk or a bookshelf after it is dry. With constant movement, the squares could loosen. Reglue them if this happens.)

MAGNIFICENT STAIRWAY

One of the most impressive temples is the Hieroglyphic Stairway in Copán. More than 2,200 **glyphs** (symbolic written or carved figures or characters that convey information) are inscribed on its 60 steps. The glyphs tell about the history of Copán and its rulers.

PART FIVE

SCIENCE, MATH, AND WRITING

The ancient Maya had the most advanced, highly developed system of math, calendars, and astronomy of any other ancient civilization in the New World, and quite possibly in the Old World. They kept incredibly accurate records of time, the movements of the planets, and numbers. Their astronomy observations were so accurate that the Maya calendar was as accurate as the one used today. It is believed that this obsession with accuracy came from their strong beliefs in astrology. According to Maya experts, accurate astronomical observations and records were needed to support their religious beliefs. Experts have suggested that this attention to detail enabled the Maya to communicate with their gods, which dominated all aspects of Maya life. The Maya believed that the sun, moon, planets, and stars were gods, and that if they observed and tracked the activities of these gods, the gods would help the Maya avoid disasters, know the right time to go to war, the best time to plant crops, and choose the best dates for ceremonies. The Maya even arranged their city buildings to align with the sun, moon, and planets.

MATH

The ancient Maya had a number system in place by A.D. 200. They used a base 20 system of counting. (The decimal system is a base 10 counting system.) The Maya, along with the ancient Babylonians and the ancient Hindus from India, was one of the few early civilizations that used the concept of zero. Because the Maya used zeros, they were able to write and calculate large numbers. Dots, rectangular-shaped bars, and a shell image represented the numbers. The shell image stood for zero, dots represented 1 through 4, and the bar represented 5. Different combinations of bars and dots represented 6 through 19.

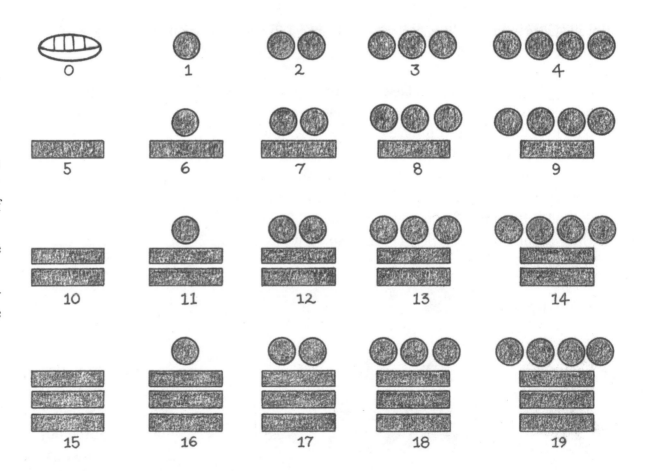

Maya Math Lesson

Learning Maya math was not that hard. The bars and dots enabled the Maya to quickly count or calculate any number problem. Maya merchants could figure out the change owed to someone by laying cacao beans and corn kernels on the ground to represent the dots and bars, then adding or subtracting to get the right change or the correct total amount due.

Since the Maya numbers are base 20, larger numbers are written in powers of 20. For example, the number 32 could be written as 1×20 (because you have one 20) $+ 12$ (because you have twelve 1s). Thus 1×20 equals 20, and $20 + 12$ equals 32. By comparison, 32 in the decimal system would be 3×10 (because you have three 10s) $+ 2$ (because you have two 1s). So 3×10 equals 30, and $30 + 2$ equals 32. The Maya wrote their numbers in a vertical column, so 32 was written as shown here.

20's (1)   ●   20

1's (12)

$$+ \ 12$$
$$\overline{}$$
$$32$$

Place value was shown vertically with the lowest value in the bottom position and the highest at the top. In the base 20 number system, here's how place value would look:

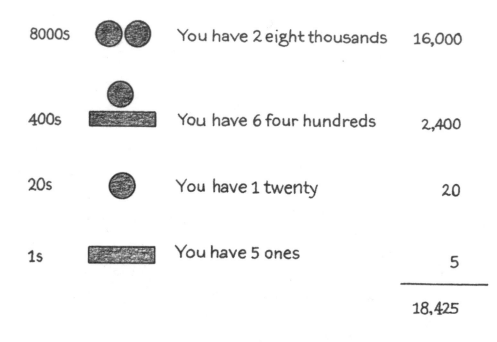

8000s	●●	You have 2 eight thousands	16,000
400s	● ▬	You have 6 four hundreds	2,400
20s	●	You have 1 twenty	20
1s	▬	You have 5 ones	5
			18,425

The bottom position represents the 1s place. Above that is the 20s place value, followed by the 400s, then the 8,000s. What place value would be above 8,000? It's easy. Here's how it's figured out. To get to the 400s place value from the 20s place value, you multiply the base 20 number by 20, so 20×20 equals 400. To get to the 8,000s place value from the

400s place value, you take the base 20 × 20 (which you did to get 400) and multiply that by 20. So, it's 20 × 20 × 20, which equals 8,000. Now it's easy to figure out the next place value. Just multiply by another 20, and you get 160,000 (20 × 20 × 20 × 20). With this formula, the Maya could calculate into the millions.

MASTER MAYA MATH

Now have fun doing some Maya math on your own.

STEPS

1 Work through the first two Maya math examples to make sure you understand the process. Once you are confident, try the other Maya math problems. It's easier if you write the numbers for each place value in a column, then add them up as you did in the example. Good luck!

Maya math examples:

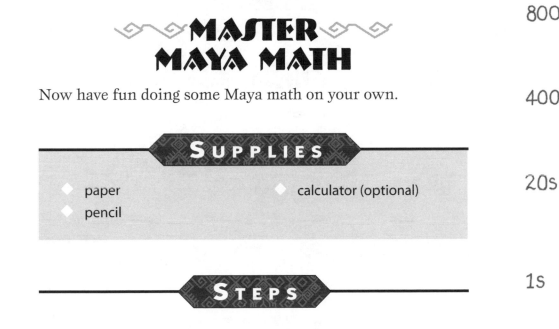

8000s		0
400s		0
20s		60
1s		+ 8
		68

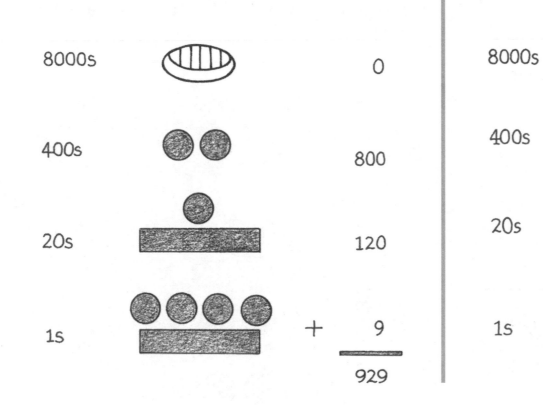

8000s	0
400s	800
20s	120
1s	+ 9
	929

(Answer on page 110.)

Maya math problem #2

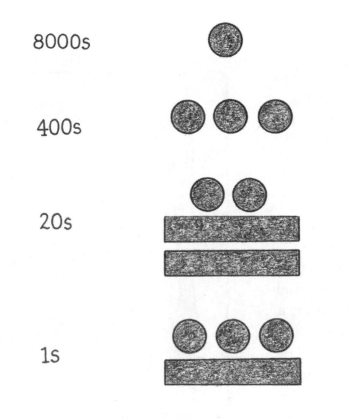

8000s

400s

20s

1s

$+$ —

(Answer on page 110.)

WRITING AND LANGUAGE

Ancient Maya writing was a complex system that used glyphs. Experts originally believed that these glyphs represented only words and concepts. But in 1952, the Russian scholar and linguist Yuri Valentinovich Knorosov suggested that the Maya glyphs represented consonant-vowel combinations to show the sounds of the Maya language. From this, experts determined that the glyphs could also represent verbs, nouns, adjectives, numbers, days, and months. For example, a glyph representing a person's name might be drawn as a cluster of glyphs that stood for the phonetic sounds in that person's name. Glyphs are generally read in pairs within a grid from left to right and from top to bottom. Many of the glyphs combined picture symbols with animal images. The Maya used the glyphs for writing only, never as decoration.

This is the glyph for *balam* (jaguar).

Maya glyphs appeared on many objects and structures throughout the empire. Buildings, temples, tombs, works of art, codices, stelae, and murals all contained glyphs. The glyphs described rulers' histories, information about the city-states, wars, and astronomical and astrological information. Works of art often bore the name of the artist in glyph.

Keepers of the Glyphs

Maya **scribes** (official writers) held a prominent place in society because few people in ancient Maya society could read or write. These keepers of information wrote or painted glyphs in codices using **quills** (stiff feathers from the wing or tail) or animal-hair brushes, or carved glyphs in stone. Scribes apprenticed for several years before they were ready to do the job on their own. Considered upper class, they lived in luxury, wore special clothes, and were generally related to the current king. Their title, *ah ts'ib,* meant "he of writing," although evidence suggests that scribes could be women, as well.

Scribes weren't just writers. They also had the important job of preserving the power of the king through writing. In many ways, they were the publicists of the ancient world. They sang the praises of the king through glyphs and made the king's accomplishments seem great indeed. If a scribe was captured by an enemy city-state, the ruler made it a point to humiliate the scribe. Scribes were stripped of their clothes except for a loincloth, paraded in front of the people, and tortured. The enemy might break the scribe's fingers, pull out his fingernails, or have him killed. The disfiguring of the fingers was extremely important because it would deprive the scribe of performing the one job for which he was honored. Even if a scribe escaped with his life, he could never write again.

Glyphs and Their Sounds

There are only about 30 vowel and consonant sounds in the Maya language. Each sound had its own glyph, and sound blends could also be represented by glyphs.

The sounds of the vowels and consonants are easy. Look at the list of Maya vowels below.

a sounds like "ah" as in *calm*

e sounds like "eh" as in *left*

i sounds like "ee" as in *seen*

o sounds like "oh" as in *bone*

oo also sounds like "oh" as in *bone,* but is held longer when spoken

u sounds like "oo" as in *soon*

Maya consonants are pronounced in the same way as consonants in the English language, except for *x*. The Maya sound for *x* is "sh" as in *shut*. The Maya did not have consonant sounds for *D, F, G, J, Q, R,* or *V*.

A crop mark, ', indicates a sudden stop between sounds.

With this pronunciation guide, it is not difficult to pronounce some simple Maya phrases. Here are a few to try:

English phrase: "Hi, how are you?"

Maya phrase: *"Bix a belex?"* (Pronunciation: Beesh ah beh-lehsh?)

English Phrase: "I'm fine."

Maya Phrase: *"Maloob."* (Pronunciation: Mah-lohb. Remember to hold the "oh" sound a little longer.)

English phrase: "Thank you."

Maya phrase: *"Yum botic."* (Pronunciation: Yoom boh-teek.)

English phrase: "You're welcome."

Maya phrase: *"Mixba."* (Pronunciation: Meesh-bah.)

(The pronunciations given here are in Yucatec Maya.)

A Fine Art

Drawing the glyphs that represented letter sounds and words was quite a challenge. The glyphs were complex and contained many artistic elements. Here are a few examples along with their meanings.

Paper Rubbings

By learning more about the glyphs and their elements, archeologists have been able to understand more about the ancient

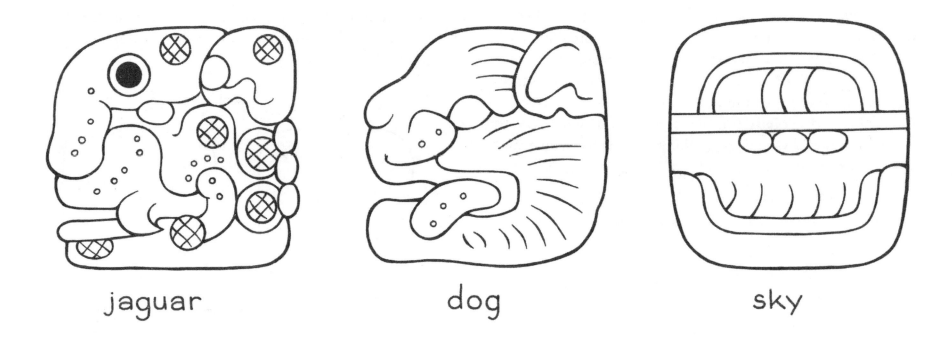

jaguar
dog
sky

Maya. In 1962, Merle Greene Robertson visited Guatemala to see the Tikal ruins and ended up staying a lot longer. She became involved in the archeological work going on at that time and made paper rubbings of the monument carvings and glyphs. Her work impressed the experts to such an extent that they asked her to make additional rubbings at other sites. Her work greatly contributed to our understanding of the ancient Maya. You can view her rubbings at this Web site: www.mesoweb.com/pari/index.html. Select Rubbings. Then select View the Rubbings.

PERSONAL GLYPH RUBBING

Use your artistic talents to create your own personal glyph rubbing. First draw the glyph on paper. Then, carve your glyph on the surface of a piece of clay. Finally, make a rubbing of your carved glyph.

If you have access to the Internet at home, in school, or at the library, use the Web site listed in Step 2 of the activity to see all the letter sounds that the glyphs represent. By breaking up your name into sounds, you can choose the glyphs that best represent your name. Some sounds have more than one glyph representation. Choose the one you like best. (Remember, the consonants *D, F, G, J, Q, R,* and *V* have no representative sounds, so you might have to substitute or leave off that sound.) If you don't have Internet access, be imaginative and create your own personal glyph. I'll use my name as an example of how to do this.

Author's name: Arlette

Maya pronunciation: Ah leht (Remember, there was no *R* sound.)

My name in glyph would be written this way:

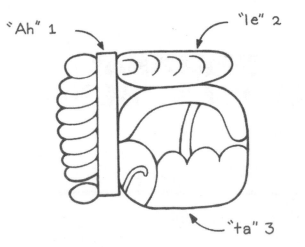

The last vowel is dropped.

It is important to cluster the sounds together to make the word. Here is a chart to show a few examples of how to order the sounds in clusters.

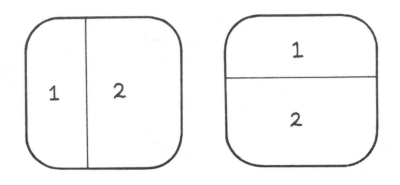

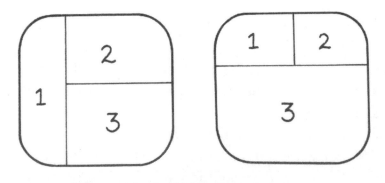

Different orders in which to cluster glyphs.

Now try your own name and make a glyph rubbing.

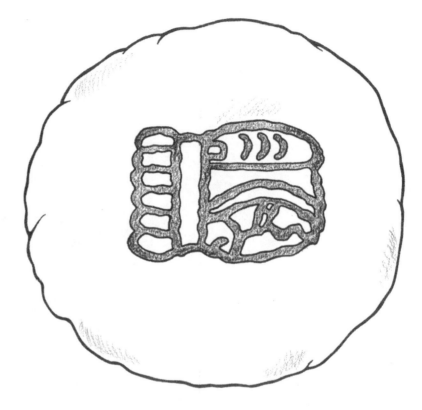

SUPPLIES

- 1 piece of scrap paper
- pencil
- self- or water-hardening craft clay
- carving tool for clay
- 1 sheet of white paper

STEPS

1 Print your name on the scrap paper. Then print your name phonetically (based on the Maya sounds for letters) as I did in the above example.

2 Here's the Web site that gives you a chart of all the glyphs represented by vowel sounds and combinations of sounds: www.famsi.org. Select Maya Writing. Then select Syllabary 2.

3 Find the specific sounds that represent your name phonetically and draw them according to the order chart shown previously.

4 Roll a piece of clay into a ball, then flatten it into a pancake with a thickness of about ¼ inch (.5 cm) and a diameter of about 4 inches (10 cm). Use the carving tool to carve your glyph into the surface of the clay. If the

spaces in the carving start to close up, gently pry them open with the pointed end of the carving tool.

5 Let the carved glyph dry according to the directions that came with your clay. After the clay has dried, place the piece of white paper over the surface and lightly rub the side of the pencil point over the surface of the paper. Your glyph will show through the rubbing.

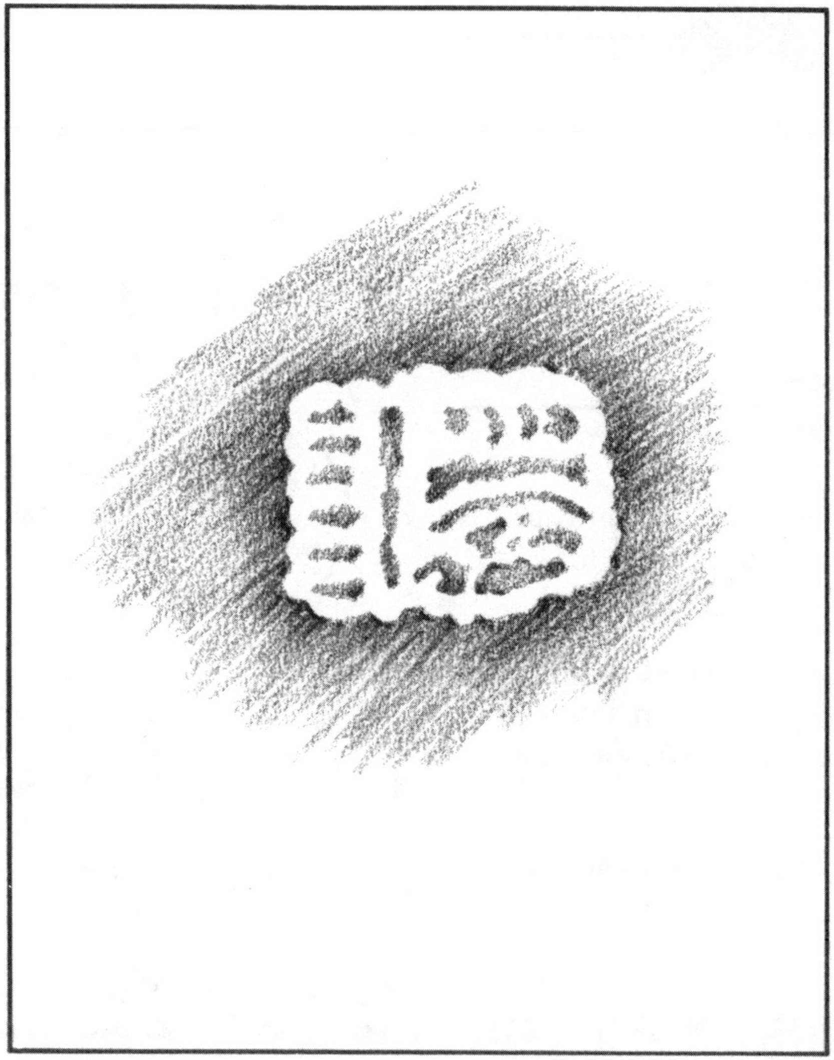

BOOKS

The Maya created codices that served as a record of their history. Only scribes performed this important job. These books, which were folded like an accordion, used paper made from the bark of the fig tree. The scribe wrote or painted glyphs on the paper using animal-hair brushes. Paints in yellow, blue, white, and brown added color to the pages and related to specific gods, nature, and the cosmos. After a codex had been written and folded, it was sometimes covered in jaguar skins.

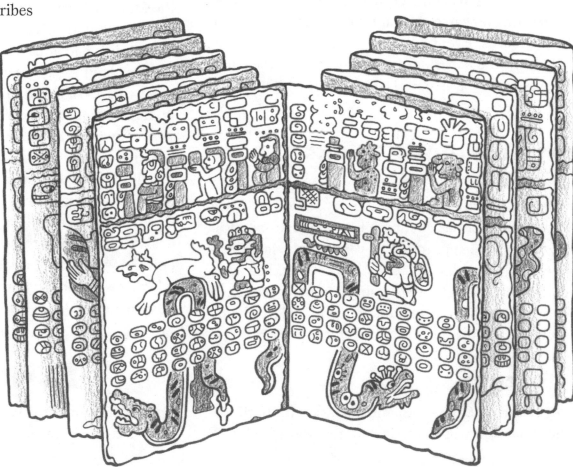

Making Book Paper

To make paper, the Maya papermakers first stripped the bark off some fig trees. They took the inner part of the bark strips and made them soft and pliable by wrapping them in a layer of banana leaves and then steaming them over a fire. After this step, the papermakers beat the soft bark with stones that had grooved surfaces. This helped to tightly mesh the bark fibers. This step was repeated several times using stones with finer and finer grooves. Eventually, the paper became smooth and strong. Finally, the papermakers lightly covered the paper with a thin layer of lime wash or plaster, which whitened the surface.

Ancient Reference Books

The codices contained information about many topics. Some told about ceremonial rituals and when they should take place. Others contained predictions about the future or astronomical information, such as the appearance of Venus in the heavens and eclipses of the sun and moon. Codices also described agricultural techniques, hunting rituals, using a firestick to make fire, beekeeping, traveling information, when to make offerings to the deities, rainmaking, and much more.

Gone Forever

In 1562, Frey Diego de Landa, a Spanish missionary to the Yucatan whose mission was to convert all the Maya to Christianity, did something that would destroy a civilization's entire literary record. He had all of the Maya codices burned, because he believed the Maya were continuing to practice their native rituals and he wanted to punish them. He also feared what King Ferdinand and Queen Isabella of Spain would do to him if they found out the Maya were not practicing Christianity. De Landa's act caused enormous distress to the Maya and was criticized by the bishop of Yucatan, who reported the priest's actions to the Spanish king. To make up for what he had done, de Landa wrote down as much information about the Maya as he could, including all the glyphs. Later this book would prove a critical stepping-stone to understanding the meaning of the glyphs.

Today there are only four codices still in existence. The Dresden Codex, perhaps one of the most beautiful, is about rituals of the gods connected with the 260-day calendar. The Madrid Codex is about agricultural rites and rituals. The Paris Codex contains astrological information. The Grolier Codex deals with the planet Venus. The codices were named for the cities in which they reside, except for the Grolier Codex, which was exhibited at the Grolier Club in New York. It is now in a museum in Mexico.

 **FAMILY CODEX**

To keep a record of your family's important events, you can make a codex in the style of the Maya codices.

- 1 sheet of paper 8½ by 11 inches (22 by 28 cm)
- tape
- scissors
- pencil
- ruler
- colored markers

STEPS

1 Fold the paper in half along the long edge. Cut on the fold. Place two of the short edges together and tape them together.

2 Along one of the long edges, make one mark about 4½ inches (11.5 cm) from one of the short edges. Fold the paper on that mark first, then like an accordion as shown.

3 The top section of the folded codex is the front cover and the bottom section of the codex is the back cover. You can decorate the covers now or after you finish the codex. You may

choose to use glyphs, have the cover look like jaguar skin, or create your own design.

4 Open the codex and lay it flat on the table.

5 Use glyphs, or pictures, to record family events you'd like to remember. (See page 92 for information on writing glyphs.) These might be a special vacation, a favorite holiday, the birth of a sister or brother, an award you won, or anything that has meaning to you. Each section of paper should have one event recorded.

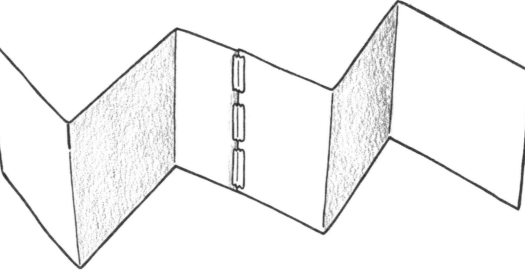

Fold paper like an accordion.

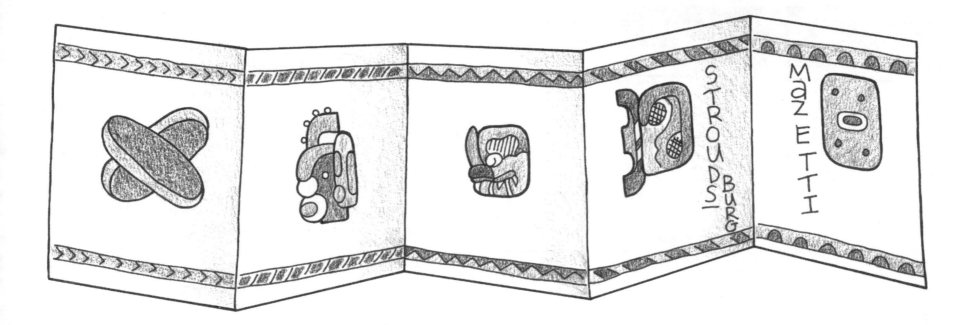

CALENDAR

The Maya calendar system was used for astrological **divination** (the practice of foretelling future events with the help of supernatural powers). Each day and number on the calendar represented a specific god or goddess, and that deity was believed to have direct influence over that day. The Maya built special observatories so that they could track the motions of the sun, moon, planets, and stars. Maya priests had the job of observing the heavens, especially the sun's rising and setting positions and the movements of the planets. Astronomical observations helped the Maya determine the best time to plant, conduct sacrifices, travel for trade, and other important life activities. Maya kings often planned their military campaigns for when the planet Venus shone brightly in the western sky, because Venus was associated with war. All of these important dates became part of the Maya calendar system.

Three Calendars

The Maya actually invented three calendars. There is some evidence to suggest that the Zapotec invented the essential elements of the Mesoamerican calendar that was used and further refined by the Maya and other civilizations.

The Sacred Count, or *tzolk'in,* was a calendar that counted days. It had 20 day names and 13 numbers and was based on a cycle of 260 days. The first day would be read as 1 Akbal (1 for the number and Akbal for the day name). Priests used this calendar to predict the future, plan rituals, and to identify lucky and unlucky dates. People would ask the priests to consult this calendar before planning important events in their lives.

The Maya Vague Year, or *haab,* was the solar calendar with 365 days and was based on the orbit of the earth around the sun. It contained 18 months with 20 days per month. The five extra days made up a short month added to the end of the year, and these days were considered unlucky. Each month had its own name.

Both the Sacred Count and the Vague Year calendars fit together like gears in a clock. Picture them as two separate wheels that fit together when turned. As the wheels turned, they created a combined date much like modern-day dates that give the name of the weekday and the name of the month

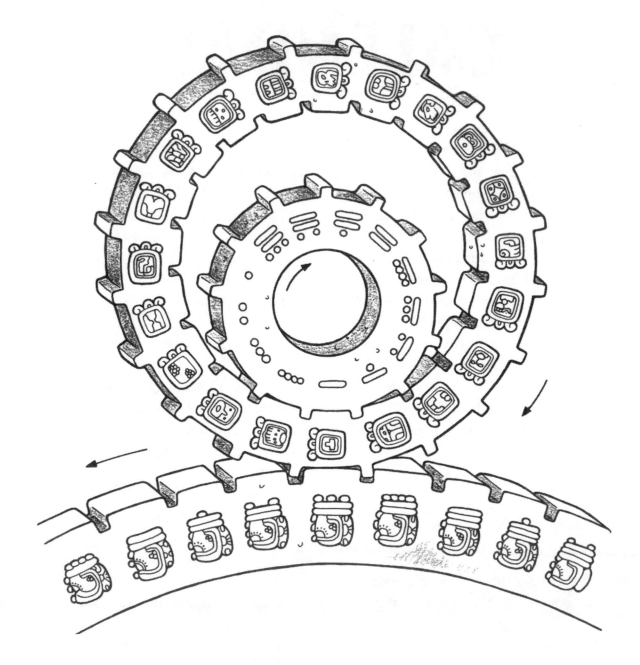

with the numbered day of the month. The starting point for each of these Maya calendars would be represented by the number 1 followed by a glyph from each calendar. Day 1 would not reappear until 18,980 days, or 52 years, had passed. This system was known as the Calendar Round.

The third calendar, the Long Count, was developed as a system for tracking the number of days that had elapsed since the beginning of their time, which is written as 0.0.0.0.1. Researchers believe the first Maya date corresponds to August 13, 3114 B.C., in our calendar. That would be the day the Maya believe that their people began. The Maya were one of the few civilizations to choose a date when they began as a people.

END-OF-THE-WORLD DATE?

The Long Count is a cycle that lasts for 1,872,000 days. Supposedly, the Long Count will end at the end of this cycle. Some researchers guess that the Maya believed that date to be the end of the world. If you calculate 1,872,000 days from the beginning date of 3114 B.C., you end up with the date December 23, 2012, in our calendar. Did the Maya believe that this would be the end of time? New evidence has shown that one Maya king predicted that his coronation would still be celebrated at the end of an 8,000-year cycle. In our calendar, that date would be 4772, many years after the 2012 end-of-the-world date. Many Long Count dates have been found carved into stone stelae and written in codices.

Old World Influence?

Some researchers think that the Maya civilization may have been influenced by ancient Asian travelers to Mesoamerica. But most scoff at this idea. No Old World artifacts have ever been found in any Maya archeological site to date. However, similarities between the named days of the 260-day Maya calendar and the Asian and Southeast Asian lunar zodiacs are striking. The similarities include a list of animals that can be matched in a similar sequence between the Maya calendar and the Asian zodiacs. Also, the Asian and the Mesoamerican cosmological systems are extremely similar in that they feature four cardinal points associated with specific plants, animals, colors, and gods. Both also see a rabbit on the face of a full moon. Another extraordinary example is that both the Maya and the Chinese astronomers of the Han Dynasty used exactly the same complex calculations to warn about solar and lunar eclipses.

BIRTHDAY GLYPH AMULET

If you have access to the Internet, you can go to a Web site that has a date converter that you can use to figure out what your birthday would be as a Maya date. Go to: www.michielb.nl/maya/calendar.html and scroll down

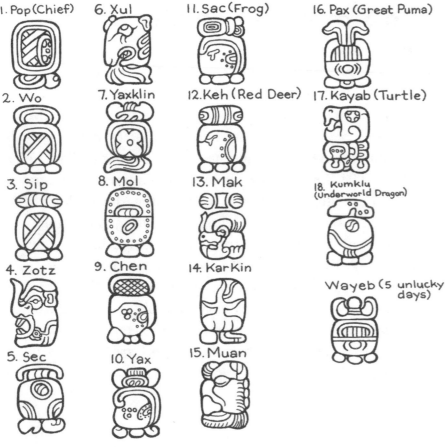

1. Pop (Chief)
2. Wo
3. Sip
4. Zotz
5. Sec
6. Xul
7. Yaxklin
8. Mol
9. Chen
10. Yax
11. Sac (Frog)
12. Keh (Red Deer)
13. Mak
14. KarKin
15. Muan
16. Pax (Great Puma)
17. Kayab (Turtle)
18. Kumklu (Underworld Dragon)
Wayeb (5 unlucky days)

determining your birthday glyph or do both if you like. See the glyphs shown here. (Note: The hieroglyph month names on the Web site may not be spelled exactly as the names shown here, but you will be able to match them up.) Once you get the glyph of your date, you can create an amulet of your Maya birthday. If you don't have access to a computer, figure out the number of your birth month, then count down to that month in the picture shown here. For example, if you were born in March (the third month in our calendar) you would count down to the third hieroglyph, or Sip (Cloud Serpent). You would use that glyph for your amulet.

SUPPLIES

- self- or water-hardening craft clay
- clay-modeling tool
- small bowl of water
- paper towels
- 1 piece of rawhide lacing, string, or yarn about 24 inches (61 cm) long
- ruler
- scissors

about three-quarters of the way on the page to the date converter. All you need to do is type in your birthday, birth month, and birth year and select "Convert" to get your Maya date and hieroglyph. The converter will show you two number/name combinations. The first number/name represents the day name and the second number/name corresponds to the month name. Use the second, or month, name for

STEPS

1 Mold a piece of clay into a flat circle with a diameter of 2 inches (5 cm) and a thickness of about $1/4$ inch (.5 cm). This is your amulet.

2 Use the pointed end of your modeling tool to carve your birthday glyph into the amulet.

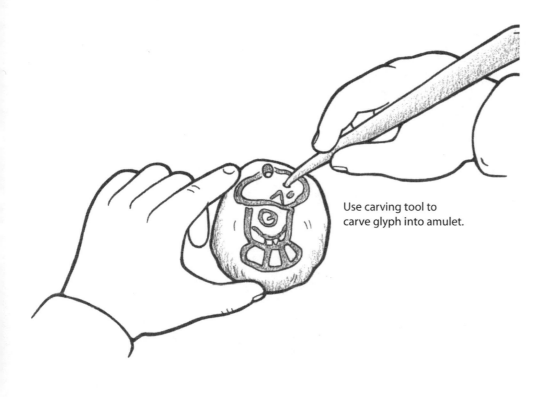

Use carving tool to carve glyph into amulet.

3 Poke a hole through the amulet near the top. Let the amulet harden according to the directions that came with the clay.

4 Cut a piece of rawhide, string, or yarn about 24 inches (61 cm) long, push one end through the top hole in the amulet, then tie the cut ends of the string together in a tight knot.

GLOSSARY

adobe   Sun-dried clay.

agave   A succulent plant related to the lily family.

aqueduct   A channel for water.

basalt   A volcanic stone.

cassava   A tropical plant grown for its fleshy edible roots.

causeway   A raised surface across wet ground or water.

cenote   A deep sinkhole in limestone with a pool of water at the bottom.

circumference   The distance around an object.

cistern   An artificial reservoir for water.

cochineal   A tiny red insect that lives in the prickly pear.

codex   An ancient book.

conch   A large spiral-shelled mollusk.

deity   A god.

dialect   A regional variety of a language that has different features from other varieties of the same language.

divination   The practice of foretelling future events with the help of supernatural powers.

elder   A person in authority because of age.

elite   A ruling class.

extinct   No longer existing.

facade   The front of a building.

fire   To heat pottery in an oven called a kiln.

fresco   The art of painting on moist lime plaster with water-based pigments.

game   Animals caught in hunting for food or sport.

glyph   A symbolic written or carved figure or character that conveys information.

horoscope   An astrological forecast.

inlaid   Decorated with a pattern set into the surface.

incense burner   A container for a material that when burned produces a fragrant odor.

indigo   A blue dye obtained from plants.

latrine   An outside bathroom.

lime   Calcium oxide.

maize   Corn.

marinate   To steep in a liquid to enhance flavor.

mason   A worker who builds with brick or stone.

Mesoamerica   Mexico and Central America.

milpas   Cornfields.

mosaic   A decoration made by placing small pieces of different-colored material on a surface to form a pattern.

obsidian   A hard volcanic rock.

pigment   A powdered substance mixed with liquid; used to color other materials.

quill   A stiff feather from the wing or tail.

sarcophagus   A stone coffin.

scribe   An official writer.

stelae   Standing stone columns.

stucco   A durable finish for exterior or interior walls; usually made of cement, sand, and lime.

tamale   Cornmeal dough rolled with a filling of ground meat or beans seasoned with chili, wrapped in corn husks, and steamed.

tapir   An animal found in tropical America.

tread   The horizontal surface area of a step.

warp   The stationary strands on a loom.

weft   The strands that are woven into the warp.

Maya Math Problem Answers

Problem 1:   2,002

Problem 2:   9,448

INDEX